Tucholsky Wagner Zola Scott Sydow Freud Schlegel
Turgenev Fonatne Wallace
Twain Walther von der Vogelweide Fouqué Friedrich II. von Preußen Freiligrath
Weber Kant Ernst Frey
Fechner Fichte Weiße Rose von Fallersleben Richthofen Frommel
Engels Fielding Hölderlin
Fehrs Faber Flaubert Eichendorff Tacitus Dumas
Feuerbach Maximilian I. von Habsburg Fock Eliasberg Zweig Ebner Eschenbach
Ewald Eliot Vergil
Goethe London
Mendelssohn Balzac Shakespeare Elisabeth von Österreich Dostojewski Ganghofer
Lichtenberg Rathenau Doyle Gjellerup
Trackl Stevenson Hambruch
Mommsen Tolstoi Lenz Droste-Hülshoff
Thoma Hanrieder
Dach Verne von Arnim Hägele Hauff Humboldt
Karrillon Reuter Rousseau Hagen Hauptmann Gautier
Garschin Defoe Baudelaire
Damaschke Descartes Hebbel
Hegel Kussmaul Herder
Wolfram von Eschenbach Darwin Dickens Schopenhauer Rilke George
Bronner Melville Grimm Jerome
Campe Horváth Aristoteles Bebel Proust
Bismarck Vigny Barlach Voltaire Federer Herodot
Gengenbach Heine
Storm Casanova Tersteegen Grillparzer Georgy
Chamberlain Lessing Langbein Gilm Gryphius
Brentano Lafontaine
Strachwitz Claudius Schiller Kralik Iffland Sokrates
Katharina II. von Rußland Bellamy Schilling
Gerstäcker Raabe Gibbon Tschechow
Löns Hesse Hoffmann Gogol Wilde Vulpius
Luther Heym Hofmannsthal Gleim
Roth Klee Hölty Morgenstern Goedicke
Heyse Klopstock Kleist
Luxemburg Puschkin Homer Mörike
Machiavelli La Roche Horaz Musil
Navarra Aurel Musset Kierkegaard Kraft Kraus
Nestroy Lamprecht Kind Kirchhoff Hugo Moltke
Marie de France
Laotse Ipsen Liebknecht
Nietzsche Nansen Ringelnatz
Marx Lassalle Gorki Klett Leibniz
von Ossietzky May vom Stein Lawrence Irving
Petalozzi Knigge
Platon Pückler Michelangelo Kafka
Sachs Poe Kock
Liebermann Korolenko
de Sade Praetorius Mistral Zetkin

The publishing house tredition has created the series **TREDITION CLASSICS**. It contains classical literature works from over two thousand years. Most of these titles have been out of print and off the bookstore shelves for decades.

The book series is intended to preserve the cultural legacy and to promote the timeless works of classical literature. As a reader of a **TREDITION CLASSICS** book, the reader supports the mission to save many of the amazing works of world literature from oblivion.

The symbol of **TREDITION CLASSICS** is Johannes Gutenberg (1400 – 1468), the inventor of movable type printing.

With the series, tredition intends to make thousands of international literature classics available in printed format again – worldwide.

All books are available at book retailers worldwide in paperback and in hardcover. For more information please visit: www.tredition.com

tredition was established in 2006 by Sandra Latusseck and Soenke Schulz. Based in Hamburg, Germany, tredition offers publishing solutions to authors and publishing houses, combined with worldwide distribution of printed and digital book content. tredition is uniquely positioned to enable authors and publishing houses to create books on their own terms and without conventional manufacturing risks.

For more information please visit: www.tredition.com

Mother Earth Land Grants in Virginia 1607-1699

Walter Stitt Robinson

Imprint

This book is part of the TREDITION CLASSICS series.

Author: Walter Stitt Robinson
Cover design: toepferschumann, Berlin (Germany)

Publisher: tredition GmbH, Hamburg (Germany)
ISBN: 978-3-8491-6653-3

www.tredition.com
www.tredition.de

CHAPTER ONE

The Land and the Indian

Among the motives for English colonization of America in the seventeenth century, the desire for free land occupied a prominent place. The availability of land in the New World appealed to all classes and ranks in Europe, particularly to the small landholder who sought to increase his landed estate and to the artisans and tenants who longed to enter the ranks of the freeholder.

The desire for land and the opportunity to provide a home for one's family, according to Professor C. M. Andrews, "probably influenced the largest number of those who settled in North America." Land also had its appeal as the gateway to freedom, contributing substantially to the shaping of the American character. When analyzing the factors that helped make this "new man, who acts upon new principles," De Crèvecoeur in 1782 emphasized the opportunity to "become a free man, invested with lands, to which every municipal blessing is annexed!"

Formulation of a land policy confronted the officials of all the colonies in early America. Its importance is reflected in the statement by C. L. Raper in his study of English colonial government that the "System and policy concerning land determine to a very considerable extent the economic, social, and political life of the colonists." The existence of the American frontier with unoccupied land was a potent force in America, and Frederick Jackson Turner stated in his famous essay in 1893 that the "Most significant thing about the American frontier is, that it lies at the hither edge of free land."

Before analyzing the nature of landholding and the land policy that was adopted in early Virginia, let us examine first the problem that arose by virtue of the presence of the Indians in North America.

At the time of the settlement of Jamestown in 1607 the area of present-day Virginia was occupied by Indians of three linguistic stocks: Algonquin, Siouan, and Iroquoian. Generally speaking, the Algonquins which included the Powhatan Confederacy inhabited the Tidewater, reaching from the Potomac to the James River and extending to the Eastern Shore. The Siouan tribes, including the Monacans and the Manahoacs, occupied the Piedmont; while the

Iroquoian group, containing the independent Nottoways and Meherrins, partially surrounded the others in a rough semicircle reaching from the headwaters of the Chesapeake through the western mountains and back to the coast in the region south of the James River.

The presence of these tribes in the areas of proposed colonization confronted the colonizers of the sixteenth and seventeenth centuries with the same problem that has faced imperialists of a later date, the question of "right and title" to land. The British, like other European nations, did not recognize the sovereign right of the heathen natives but claimed a general title to the area by the prevailing doctrine of right by discovery and later by the generally accepted doctrine of effective occupation. As stated in the charter to Sir Walter Raleigh in 1584 with essentially the same provision included in the first charter of Virginia in 1606, the colonizers were authorized to occupy land "not actually possessed of any Christian Prince, nor inhabited by Christian People." Over the Indians the British maintained a "limited sovereignty"; and when acknowledging any claim, they recognized only the Indian's right of occupation and asserted the "exclusive right" to extinguish this title which occupancy gave them.

In the first years of the colony not even these tenure rights were recognized by the British. While a few gifts of land had been made by the natives and one of these confirmed by the London Company, there was no admission, either direct or by inference, that the Indians possessed a superior claim to the land. When such an implication was made in a land grant to Barkham in 1621, the company reacted with bitter resentment. Governor Yeardley, striving to maintain peace with the natives, made the grant conditional upon the consent of the Indian chief Opechancanough. According to stated practice under the company, the grant then had to be approved in England by a quarter court of the company's stockholders. When Barkham's petition was presented for ratification, the members of the court held the provision concerning the Indian chief to be "verie dishonorable and prejudiciall" for it infringed upon the company's title by acknowledging sovereignty in that "heathen infidell."

Disregard for the aboriginal occupants of Virginia called forth anew the question of "right and title," a problem subject to discussion in England even before Jamestown. To allay these attacks, several proponents of colonial expansion attempted to justify the policy of the crown and the London Company.

Sir George Peckham in *A true reporte of the late discoveries* pointed out as early as 1583, relating to the discoveries of Sir Humphrey Gilbert, that it was "lawfull and necessary to trade and traficke with the savages." In a series of subsequent arguments, he then expounded the right of settlement among the natives and the mutual benefit to them and to England. This theme was later extended by the author of *Nova Britannia*, who maintained that the object of the English was to settle in the Indian's country, "yet not to supplant and roote them out, but to bring them from their base condition to a farre better" by teaching them the "arts of civility." The author of *Good Speed to Virginia* added that the "Savages have no particular propertie in any part or parcell of that countrey, but only a generall residencie there, as wild beasts have in the forests." This last opinion, according to Philip A. Bruce, prevailed to a great extent and was held by a majority of the members of the London Company in regard to the appropriations of lands.

In spite of these views entertained by the company, there were several instances in which the natives were compensated for their territory. This was done primarily through the initiative of local authorities, for they were usually better informed concerning Indian affairs. They were in much closer contact with the natives than the company's Council in London and realized that the goodwill of the aborigines could be cultivated by giving only minor considerations for the land occupied by the English. On other occasions the Indians voluntarily gave up their land such as the present from Opechancanough in 1617 of a large body of land at Weyanoke. At still other times land was seized by force. When any attempt was made to justify the seizure, it was done on the basis of an indemnity for damage inflicted upon the colony or for violations of agreements by the natives. By 1622 settlements had been made along the banks of the lower James River and in Accomac on the Eastern Shore, the land having been obtained by direct purchase, by gifts from the natives, or by conquest.

Any attempt to determine the extent of the areas acquired by purchase in Virginia is hindered by the indefinite nature of the Indian holdings and by the lack of complete records for the early periods. Thomas Jefferson thought much of the land had been purchased. Writing to St. George Tucker in 1798, Jefferson stated:

At an early part of my life, from 1762 to 1775, I passed much time in going through the public records in Virginia, then in the secretary's office, and especially those of a very early date of our settlement. In these are abundant instances of purchases made by our first assemblies of the indi[ans] around them. The opinion I formed at the time was that if the records were complete & thoroughly searched, it would be found that nearly the whole of the lower country was covered by these contracts.

Jefferson overestimated the amount of land that was purchased by Virginia during the early years. While the records now extant show that the colony often purchased lands, they likewise indicate that frequently land was appropriated without compensation. Especially during the years following the first massacre of 1622, "The Indians were stripped of their inheritance without the shadow of justice." The greater part of the Peninsula between the York and James rivers was taken by conquest; the right of possession was later confirmed by a treaty with Necotowance in 1646, without, however, any stipulation for compensating the natives for the land they relinquished.

The treaty of 1646 with the successor of Opechancanough inaugurated the policy of major historical significance of either setting aside areas reserved for Indian tribes, or establishing a general boundary line between white and Indian settlements. Influenced by the desire of individual settlers to fortify their claims and by the opposition of the natives to white encroachment, the colony designated definite lands for the Virginia Indians and began to follow more closely the custom of purchasing all territory received from the natives. To see that this was done, the Assembly passed numerous laws, pertaining in most cases only to the specific tribes of Indians mentioned in each act.

In 1653 the Assembly ordered that the commissioners of York County remove any persons then seated upon the territory of the

Pamunkey or Chickahominy Indians. At the same time both lands and hunting grounds were assigned to the red men of Gloucester and Lancaster counties. The following year the Indian tribes of Northampton County on the Eastern Shore were granted the right to sell their land to the English provided a majority of the inhabitants of the Indian town consented and provided the Governor and Council of the colony ratified the procedure. Soon other tribes were given the same privilege. So anxious were they to dispose of their land when allowed to convey a legal title, that it became necessary for the colony to forbid further land transfers without the Assembly's stamp of approval. Such a step was taken in order to prevent the continual necessity of apportioning new lands to keep the natives satisfied.

By 1658 the Assembly had received from several Indian tribes so many complaints of being deprived of their land, either by force or fraud, that measures were again adopted to protect the natives in their rights. No member of the colony was allowed to occupy lands claimed by the natives without consent from the Governor and Council or from the commissioners of the territory where the settlement was intended. To decrease the chances for cheating the Indians, all sales were to be consummated at quarter courts where unfair purchases could be prevented.

Efforts to protect the Indians in the possession of their lands were subject to modification from time to time. The treaty of 1646 designated the York River as the line to separate the settlements of the English and the natives. But the colony at that time was on the eve of a great period of expansion. With an estimated population of 15,000 in 1650, the colony increased by 1666 to approximately 40,000, and by 1681 to approximately 80,000. To stem the tide of the advancing English settlement was apparently an impossibility. Therefore, Governor William Berkeley and the Council, upon representation from the Burgesses, consented to the opening of the land north of the York and Rappahannock rivers after 1649. At the same time the provision making it a felony for the English to go north of the York was repealed. This turn in policy, based upon the assumption that some intermingling of the white and red men was inevitable, led to the effort to provide for an "equitable division" of land supplemented by attempts to modify the Indian economy which had previously demanded vast areas of the country.

Endeavoring to provide for this "equitable division" of land, the Assembly in 1658 forbade further grants of lands to any Englishmen whatsoever until the Indians had been allotted a proportion of fifty acres for each bowman. The land for each Indian town was to lie together and to include all waste and unfenced land for the purpose of hunting. This provision did not relieve all pressure on Indians' lands, partly because some of the natives never received their full proportion and partly because some had been accustomed to even larger areas. But it did serve as a basis for reservation of land for different tribes.

From a portrait reproduced in J. H. Claiborne, *William Claiborne of Virginia*.
Photo by Flournoy, Virginia State Chamber of Commerce.

William Claiborne, Surveyor for Virginia, Secretary of the Colony of Virginia

How to reduce all sorts of grounds into a square for the better measuring of it.

From John Norden's "Surveior's Dialogue"
Photo by T. L. Williams

Two years later the Assembly in 1660 took definite steps to relieve the pressure of English encroachments upon the territory of the Accomac Indians on the Eastern Shore. Enough land was assigned to the natives of Accomac to afford ample provisions for subsistence over and above the supplies that might be obtained through hunting and fishing. To insure a fair and just distribution of these lands, the Assembly passed over surveyors of the Eastern Shore and required that the work be done by a resident of the mainland, who obviously would be less prejudiced against the aborigines because of personal interest. When once assigned to the natives, the land could not be alienated.

By 1662 this last provision, forbidding the Accomacs to alienate their lands, was extended to all Indians in Virginia. The Assembly had realized that the chief cause of trouble was the encroachment by the whites upon Indian territory. Efforts, therefore, had been made to remove this cause of friction by permitting purchases from the natives provided each sale was publicly announced before a quarter court or the Assembly. But the plan had not been a complete success. Various members of the colony had employed all kinds of ingenious devices to persuade the natives to announce in public their willingness to part with their land. Dishonest interpreters had rendered "them willing to surrender when indeed they intended to have received a confirmation of their owne rights." In view of these evil practices the Assembly declared all future sales to be null and void.

Twenty-eight years later in 1690 the Governor and Council in accord with this restriction nullified several purchases made from the Chickahominy Indians. By order of the Assembly in 1660 this tribe had received lands in Pamunkey Neck. Since that time several colonists had either purchased a part of their land or encroached upon their territory without regard for compensation. In neither case were the white settlers allowed to remain. All leases, sales, and other exchanges were declared void by the Governor and Council, and all intruders were ordered to withdraw and burn the buildings that had been constructed. George Pagitor, being one of the settlers affected by this order, had obtained about 1,200 acres in Pamunkey Neck from the natives. He had built a forty-foot tobacco barn and kept two workers there most of the year. When his purchase was declared void, he was ordered to return the land to the natives and to burn the barn that had been constructed. Accompanying this executive decree was an order to the sheriff of New Kent County authorizing him to carry out the will of the officials of the colony and to burn the barn himself, if necessary.

Commissioners were also employed for the supervision of Indian lands. Upon the recommendation of the committee appointed for Indian affairs, the Assembly in 1662 authorized the Governor to appoint a commission "to enquire into and examine the severall claimes made to any part of our neighboring Indian land, and confirme such persons who have justly invested themselves, and cause all others to remove." The English with rights to land within three miles of the natives were to assist in fencing the Indian corn fields. This was done to prevent harm to the Indian crops by hogs and cattle of the colony. Commissioners appointed were to designate the time and number of English to aid in the construction. Other commissioners were to view annually the boundaries separating the two people.

The commissioners diligently enforced the provisions of these laws which underwent few changes until the outburst of hostilities in Bacon's Rebellion. In 1678 the additional expense of the Indian war led the colony to modify temporarily its former provisions in order to obtain more revenue from land. All territory recently assigned to the Indians but then abandoned and any land then occupied that should later be deserted were to be sold. The proceeds from the sale were to be used in the public interest to defray the expense of the war.

This regulation applied only to land abandoned by the Indians. The colony continued to protect the natives in other lands assigned them as is exemplified in the region south of the James River. In 1665 the Indian boundary line for the area was designated to run from the southern branches of the Blackwater River to the Appomattox Indian town, and from there to Manakin Town located only a few miles above the Fall Line. By 1674 some of the colonists had crossed this line and were settling on the territory of the Nottoway Indians. When the encroachment was called to the attention of the Governor and Council, they ordered the English to withdraw immediately, and in the next instructions to the surveyor of the colony they again forbade the location of new grants in the region designated as Indian land.

The number of the aborigines gradually dwindled in this section as in other parts of the colony, due mainly to wars, smallpox epidemics, spirituous liquors, migration, and the abridgement of territory of a people who lived principally on the "spontaneous productions of nature." Because of the decrease the Burgesses in 1685 appealed to Governor Howard for permission to allow grants to some of the land in the area. The Governor failed to comply with their requests. Later, in 1690, an order was issued for the immediate removal of several persons who had obtained illegal patents to land south of the main Blackwater Swamp. All members of the colony were again forbidden to settle beyond the boundary line, and any who had already constructed houses were ordered not to repair them nor to finish any other uncompleted buildings. The sheriffs and justices of the peace of Charles City, Surry, Isle of Wight, and Nansemond counties were instructed to be on the alert for violators of the order.

However, the Indians themselves, residing in the region on the south side of the Blackwater River and in Pamunkey Neck had requested in 1688 that colonists be allowed to settle across the boundary line in the area now made vacant by the gradual dying out of their tribes. The basis for the request seems to have been a desire for relief in their precarious economic condition and the fear of invasion by hostile Indians, whom they regarded with more apprehension than they did the English. By 1705, the colony, influenced by the request from the natives revoked its former law regarding the Indian boundary, permitting a limited number of white settlements in Pamunkey Neck and in the region south of the Blackwater Swamp and Nottoway River.

Thus in the seventeenth century the pendulum moved from a position of the colony ignoring any Indian rights in the land to a gradual recognition of the Indian right of occupation. This sweep of the pendulum brought the establishment of boundary lines between the whites and the Indians with reservations being designated for certain tribes. By the end of the century the diminution of the tribes found the pendulum swinging back to open the area to white settlement which had once been reserved to the natives, yet still retaining the recognition of the Indian's right of occupation where tribes survived. With this survey of the problem of the red man's title to land, let us now turn to a consideration of the white man's title and how it was obtained in seventeenth-century Virginia.

CHAPTER TWO

The London Company

General boundaries for English settlement were designated in the charter of 1606 creating the London Company and the Plymouth Company to settle the area in America known as Virginia. The London Company was authorized to settle a tract of land 100 miles square in the southern part of the area extending from the thirty-fourth to the forty-first degrees north latitude, or from the Cape Fear River in present North Carolina to New York City. The boundaries for the Plymouth Company were from the thirty-eighth to the forty-fifth degrees north latitude, or from approximately the mouth of the Potomac River to a line just north of present Bangor, Maine. In the overlapping area between the thirty-eighth and forty-first degrees, which in effect created a neutral zone between the present location of Washington, D.C., and New York City, provision was made for a distance of at least 100 miles to separate the sites that might be selected by the two companies.

As stated in the charter of 1606, "all the lands, tenements, and hereditaments" were to be held "as of our Manor at East-Greenwich in the County of Kent, in free and common soccage only, and not in capite." The "Manor at East-Greenwich" refers to the residence of King James I at the royal palace of Greenwich and was used as a descriptive term in many grants to indicate that the land in America was also considered a part of the demesne of the King. The land was held not "in fee simple" with absolute ownership, a concept which was not a part of English law at the time; but it was granted "in free and common soccage" with the holder a tenant of the King with obligations of fealty and of the payment of a quitrent. The fixed rent replaced the service, military or personal, required under feudal law; and the socage tenure in effect did not subject the land to the rules of escheat or return of the land to the King if inherited by minors or widows. For Englishmen in America, the "Instructions for the government of the colonies" in 1606 were explicit in showing that their legal and tenurial rights were the same as residents of the mother country by stating that "All the lands, tenements, and hereditaments ... shal be had and inherited and enjoyed, according as in the like estates they be had and enjoyed by the lawes within this realme of England."

Government by the charter of 1606 provided for a strong exercise of control by the crown over the colonies of both companies. This was achieved through the establishment of the Council for Virginia that was appointed by the King, was resident in England, and answered to the King through the Privy Council for its actions. For local control of each company, authorization was made for a Council in America with its initial membership determined by the Council for Virginia and with a president selected by the local group.

Few details were given either in the charter or "Instructions" of 1606 about distribution of land. Provisions did state that grants of land in the colony would be made in the name of the King to persons whom the local Council "nominate and assign"; but no details were given of the method of land distribution. From the scant records that survive, it is evident that promises of land were made to individuals who were willing to hazard the dangers of the new country. From a bill of adventure that goes back to 1608, the nature of the promise of land is revealed in the agreement between Henry Dawkes and Richard Atkinson, clerk of the Virginia Company. Fortunately the bill of adventure of 1608 was recorded with the patent by Governor John Harvey in 1632 to William Dawkes, son and heir of Henry Dawkes. The commitments in the bill of adventure were as follows:

Whereas Henry Dawkes now bound on the intended voyage to Virginia hath paid, in ready money, to Sr. Thomas Smith Kt. treasurer for Virginia the some of twelve pounds tenn shillings for his adventure in the voyage to Virginia.

It is agreed that for the same the said Henry Dawkes his heires, executors, admrs. and assignes shall have rateably according to his adventure his full pte. of all such lands tenemts and hereditamts. as shall from time to time bee there planted and inhabited, and of all such mines and minneralls of gould, silver, and other mettalls or treasures, pearles, pretious stoanes or any kinds of wares or merchandize, comodities or pfitts. whatsoever, which shal bee obtained or gotten in the said voyage, according to the portion of money by him imployed to that use, In as large and ample manner as any other adventurer therein shall receave for the like some.

Written this fowerteenth of July one thousand six hundred and eight.

Richard Atkinson
[Clerk of the Virginia Company].

The first two years at Jamestown brought disappointments, but the adventurers of the London Company found grounds for new hope in the enlarged and expanded program that was inaugurated in 1609. A new charter was sought from the King to make possible reforms in governmental organization both in England and Virginia; and a broader base for financial support was laid by inviting the public to subscribe to a joint-stock fund. By the charter of 1609 the new organization was incorporated as the Treasurer and Company of Adventurers and Planters of the City of London for the First Colony in Virginia. In England the head of the reorganized company was designated as treasurer, and the major change in control was the transfer of authority over the colony from the crown to the company with the powers of government in the hands of the treasurer and Council. This Council in England, which continued for some time to be called the Council for Virginia, had its jurisdiction limited to the exploits of the London Company; its membership came entirely from the company; and its members were in effect selected by the leading promoters of the company. One major governmental change occurred in the colony by the president and Council being eliminated in favor of a strong Governor to be advised by a Council. The former provision for title to an area of land 100 miles square was changed to give title to "all that space and circuit of land" lying 200 miles north and 200 miles south of Point Comfort from the sea coast "up into the land, throughout from sea to sea, west, and northwest" plus islands within 100 miles of the coast.

Provisions relative to distribution of land were more specific in the 1609 charter and provided that land should be conveyed by majority vote of the company under its common seal. Consideration in distribution of land was to be given both to the amount invested by adventurer as well as "special service, hazard, exploit, or merit of any person."

In the third charter of 1612 no major changes were included relative to land. Boundaries of the colony were extended from 100 miles to 300 leagues to include the newly discovered Bermuda Islands. And greater governmental authority was placed in the generality of the company by providing for quarterly court meetings of the company to handle "matters and affairs of greater weight and importance" than were resolved by lesser courts of a smaller portion of the company.

No immediate grants of land to individuals were forthcoming with these charters. Only promises were made to those who subscribed to the joint-stock undertaking. The adventurer invested only his money and remained in England with each unit of investment set at £12 10s. per share. The term planter was applied to one who went to the colony, and his personal adventure was equated to one unit of investment at the same rate as above. Both adventurer and planter were promised a proportionate share of any dividends distributed, whether in land or in money. The joint-stock arrangement was originally set to continue seven years from its inception in 1609, thus making 1616 as the terminal date. During this period monetary dividends might be declared, and at the end of the period the land suitable for cultivation was to be divided with at least 100 acres to be given for each share of stock. The tract *Nova Britannia* of 1609, written by Robert Johnson as a part of the promotional campaign of the London Company, outlined these major provisions concerning land and included the optimistic prediction that each share of £12 10s. would be worth 500 acres at least. But an attempt fourteen years later by Captain Martin to justify a patent based on this figure of 500 acres per share failed because the promise was held to be the work of a private individual and not a commitment by the court of the company.

In the absence of private title to land in the early years of the Virginia colony, the company relied upon a corporate form of management with the pooling of community effort to clear the land, construct buildings, develop agriculture, and engage in trade with the Indians. This was not an experiment based on a theory of communism for the joint-stock claims were limited in time. Most of the settlers were more in a position of contract laborers performing services for the company, and plans were devised for monetary dividends even before 1616 if the colony prospered. Inadequate supplies from England, severe weather conditions, hostility of the Indians, and the lack of willingness for industrious labor on the part of the early settlers depleted the common storehouse upon which the colonists were forced to rely, leading to the exercise of stern and autocratic measures by John Smith and some of his successors as leaders in the colony. Among the factors that contributed to the lack of zeal among the settlers was the absence of private ownership of land.

Prior to the promised distribution of land in 1616, there was granted private use of land under a tenant-farm policy which most probably was first inaugurated in 1614 under Sir Thomas Dale, although there is some uncertainty about the date. Three acres of "cleare ground" were allotted to men of the old settlement. In effect they became tenants of the company and were obligated to render only one month's service to the colony at some period other than the planting and harvesting time and to contribute annually to the common magazine two barrels and a half of corn on the ear. This tenant-farm policy worked well and better conditions resulted with increased production of crops and stock. According to one account in 1616:

They sow and reape their corne in sufficient proportion, without want or impeachment; their kine multiply already to some hundreds, their swine to many thousands, their goates and poultry in great numbers, every man hath house and ground to his owne use....

In the same year this policy was extended to include eighty-one farmers or tenants in the colony's total population of 351.

Despite improvement in the supply of provisions, the company still had to face the harsh facts that in 1616 there were only 351 persons alive in the colony, and funds were low in the treasury. There had been only a limited number of new subscribers; some of the earlier subscribers had defaulted on their second or third payments; and the use of lotteries had failed to provide adequate money. This was the year set for the end of the joint ownership of land with the declaration of land dividends. But the company could not provide the necessary funds to defray the administrative costs for the land divisions; and furthermore, many were of the opinion that not enough land in possession had been cleared of trees and surveyed. The arbitrary conduct of the Deputy Governor Captain Samuel Argall, who arrived in Virginia in May, 1617, also contributed to the delay in carrying out the plan for land distribution.

In A Briefe Declaration of the present state of things in Virginia, adventurers were told that "this course of sending a Governor with commissioners and a survayor, with men, ships, and sundry provisions" would be expensive, and plans were announced for only a preliminary or "first divident" of fifty acres with the expressed hope that a later division would bring at least 200 acres for every share. But even for the preliminary division, more money was needed and shareholders were asked to subscribe another £12 10s. to help pay for the administrative cost. For each additional subscription of £12 10s., a fifty-acre grant would be made. Here we have provisions for obtaining land by "treasury right," a method remaining in effect only until dissolution of the company in 1624 and not reappearing until 1699. Planters in the colony were also to receive a fifty-acre grant for their personal adventure. Even new adventurers were invited to buy shares at £12 10s. and were promised fifty-acre grants with the same privileges of the old adventurers. But the response was poor. Most of the grants that were made were either irregular in form or contained unreasonable provisions dictated by the exigency of the situation, thereby being later repudiated by the company.

The financial embarrassment of the company and the need for further colonization led to grants of land in return for service to the company by officials or for promoting the transportation of colonists. For the services of Sir Thomas Dale to the colony, the Council for Virginia awarded him the value of 700 pounds sterling to be received in land distribution; to Sir Thomas Smith for his noteworthy efforts as treasurer or chief official of the company, 2,000 acres; and to Captain Daniel Tucker for his aiding the colony with his pinnace and for his service as vice-admiral, fifteen shares of land. Similar rewards could be made under the company to ministers, physicians, and other government officials.

As a further stimulus to expand the population of the colony and to enhance agricultural production, the company beginning in 1617 encouraged private or voluntary associations, organized on a joint-stock basis, to establish settlements in the area of the company's patent. These "societies of adventurers" were to send to Virginia at their own expense, tenants, servants, and supplies; and the associates were given certain governmental powers over the settlement that approached the position of an independent colony. They were authorized "till a form of government is here settled over them" to issue orders and ordinances provided they were not contrary to the laws of England. In relation to the four original boroughs of James City, Charles City, Henrico, and Kecoughtan (later Elizabeth City), the hundreds or particular plantations in government were "co-ordinate and not subordinate"; and some of them sent representatives to the first Assembly held in 1619 under Governor Yeardley.

The amount of land in these sub-patents depended upon the number of shares of stock of the associates, and in effect the grants served as dividends to the shareholders. One hundred acres were granted for each share with the first division of land, and the promise was made for an equal amount upon a second division of land provided the first was "sufficiently peopled." There was to be some choice in location by the associates, although certain restrictions were imposed. No grant was to be located within five miles of the four original boroughs, and the plantation should be ten miles from other settlements unless on opposite sides of an important river. These provisions were designed to provide for expansion and at the same time avoid conflict among plantations, yet they tended to disperse the colony and complicate efforts to maintain adequate protection from the imminent threat of hostile natives.

The term hundred was applied to some, but not all, of these particular plantations. The origin of this designation has sometimes been explained as a derivation from the English administrative system, but this seems valid only as it pertains to the name. There was no attempt to establish a system based on English counties and hundreds, rather the Virginia hundreds were closer to the feudal manor with a degree of economic and political independence. In the light of these conditions, Professor Wesley Frank Craven suggested the possibility that the term might have been a "colloquial designation" applied to plantations with no definite name and related to the units of 100 acres included in the grants or by the requirement to seat 100 settlers on the land.

There were three general types of particular plantations. The first of these represented the voluntary pooling of land and resources by several adventurers of the company, since few had adequate land or financial support to go it alone. The company granted a patent to contiguous areas of land according to the number of shares of stock possessed by the group. Examples of this type include the Society of Smith's Hundred and Martin's Hundred. Smith's Hundred, later called Southampton Hundred, was organized in 1617 and included among its adventurers Sir Thomas Smith, Sir Edwin Sandys, and the Earl of Southampton. The grant included 80,000 acres and was located on the north side of the James River in the area between "Tanks Weyanoke" and the Chickahominy River. The society was administered by a treasurer and committees selected by a meeting of the adventurers. The associates settled at least 300 colonists within their boundaries and reported in 1635 the expenditure of £6,000 on the settlement. Martin's Hundred, organized in 1618, was named for Richard Martin and should be distinguished from (John) Martin's Brandon organized the previous year. The Society of Martin's Hundred held patent to 80,000 acres and dispatched over 250 colonists, but only a part of the tract was ever occupied.

The second type of particular plantation involved an adventurer who combined with persons outside the company to obtain a grant. The title usually resided in the original adventurer, and the nature of government and special privileges was similar to grants of the first kind discussed above. The grant made to Captain Samuel Argall was of this type. So was the grant of John Martin's Brandon in 1617, a plantation of 7,000 acres situated seven miles upstream from Jamestown.

The third type of grant involved new adventurers whose major purpose in buying stock in the company was to organize a particular plantation. Illustrative of this category was the plantation of Christopher Lawne, who transported 100 settlers in 1619 to Warrosquoik and established Lawne's Hundred. During the following year the hundred was dissolved and thereafter called Isle of Wight Plantation.

Beginning with the election of Sir Edwin Sandys as treasurer in 1619 and including the next four years, there were forty-four grants made for particular plantations; and the company declared six others to have been made prior to this time under Sir Thomas Smith. All of the projected plantations, however, were never located; and few were settled to the extent planned by the company. Historical records are scarce for these projects and this paucity of material has left much of the story incomplete. It is certain that the following additional plantations were actually established in Virginia: Archer's Hope on the James River, Bargrave's Settlement, Bennett's Welcome, Society of Truelove's Plantation, Persey's or Flowerdieu Hundred, and Berkeley Town or Hundred. For the last of these, Berkeley Hundred, there is an extensive set of records in the Smyth of Nibley Papers that gives considerable insight into the organization and activities of the adventurers under the leadership of Richard Berkeley, George Thorpe, William Throckmorton, and John Smyth of Nibley.

Resembling its larger prototype, the London Company, the Berkeley Hundred group had a governor and council. The adventurers were granted 100 acres of land for each share of stock with the promise of an equal amount when the first grant was settled; likewise they were promised fifty acres without quitrent for every person transported at their expense who remained for three years or died within this period. For promoting both a church and school, the adventurers were also granted 1,500 acres. With these grants and with exemptions from both the company's trade rules and from taxation except by consent, the leaders of Berkeley Hundred inaugurated a vigorous campaign to provide the necessary provisions and personnel, including farmers, artisans, overseers, a minister, and a doctor. Over ninety people were dispatched to the colony in 1619 and 1620 at a cost of approximately £2,000. This settlement, however, did not thrive. Many of the settlers died of disease and eleven were killed in the Indian massacre of 1622. By 1636 the adventurers had abandoned their plans to continue the settlement and sold their interests to London merchants.

In addition to the stimulus to migration by the three foregoing types of grants for particular plantations, the company took steps in 1618 toward reorganization of its administration. Sir Thomas Smith was still in control of the company as treasurer and contributed to the reforms, but the major contribution came from Sir Edwin Sandys who succeeded to the position of treasurer in the spring of the following year. Rules and by-laws were restated in the "Orders and Constitutions," which were largely prepared in 1618 although not formally adopted until June, 1619. One additional document of 1618 was very significant because it outlined a uniform land policy. Identified by the term "the greate charter," it is listed in the *Records* of the London Company as "Instructions to Governor Yeardly" under the date November 18, 1618.

This "charter" outlined plans for distribution of the land dividend and contained provisions for the headright system which became a basic feature of the colony's land policy. One hundred acres were promised as a first dividend to all adventurers for each paid-up share of stock at £12 10s., another 100 acres as a second dividend when the first had been settled ("sufficiently peopled"). "Ancient planters," that is, those who had come to the colony prior to the departure of Sir Thomas Dale in 1616, were to receive similar grants if they had come to the colony at their own expense. These foregoing grants were to be free of quitrent. "Ancient planters" who came to the colony at the company's expense would receive the same amount of land after a seven-year term of service but would be required to pay a quitrent of two shillings for every 100 acres.

For settlers arriving after the departure of Dale in 1616 or those migrating during the seven-year period following Midsummer Day of 1618, separate regulations applied. If transported at company expense, the colonist was to serve as a half-share tenant for seven years with no promise of a land grant; if at his own expense, he was to receive as a headright fifty acres on the first dividend and the same amount on the second dividend. This provision for the fifty-acre headright was set up for the seven-year period prior to Midsummer Day of 1625, but it continued beyond this date as the essential key to Virginia's land policy of the seventeenth century.

Out of the number of people who purchased a share in the company and thereby received a bill of adventure, Alexander Brown in his *Genesis of the United States* estimated that about one-third came to Virginia and took up their land claim; approximately one-third sent over agents, or in some cases heirs, to benefit by the grants; and the remaining one-third disposed of their shares to others who occupied the lands.

Provisions for special lands were also stated in "the greate charter." At each of the four focal points of settlement—James City, Charles City, Henrico, and Kecoughtan, 3,000 acres were to be set aside as the company's land. Half-share tenants were to cultivate the lands and half of the company's profits was to be used to support several of the colonial officials. For the Governor, a special plot known as the Governor's land was to be designated at Jamestown, and half of the proceeds of the tenants was to go to the Governor. For local government, additional provisions were made for support by setting aside 1,500 acres as "burroughs land" at the four points of settlement listed above.

Support of cultural activities, as well as governmental, was also provided by land. Glebe lands were authorized at each borough, including 100 acres for the minister with a supplement from church members to pay a total of £200 per annum. For the promotion of education, "the greate charter" set aside 10,000 acres at Henrico as an endowment for a "university and college." The primary aim of the college in 1618 was to serve as an Indian mission, although the training of English students was probably a part of the plan. Tenants were dispatched to Virginia to work at Henrico as "tenants at halves," one-half of the proceeds of their labor to go to the tenant, the other half to be used for the building of the college and for support of its tutors and students. One hundred and fifty tenants were sent over for the college land; and to improve the returns from this enterprise, Sir Edwin Sandys engaged that "worthy religious gentleman" George Thorpe as deputy to supervise the investment in the college land. Patrick Copland, projector of the first English free school in North America, was designated president-elect of the Indian college; and Richard Downes, a scholar in England, came to Virginia in 1619 with plans to work in the proposed college. All of these hopeful plans were suddenly blasted by the eruption of the

Indian massacre of 1622. For all practical purposes the project was ended, although some efforts were made after 1622 by the company to have the remaining tenants cultivate the land and to hold the bricklayers to the obligations of their contract.

The trace of these grants, including the company land, the Governor's land, and the "burroughs land" fades out in the absence of complete records for this period of the colony. Use of the glebe land as partial support for the minister was continued in later years, although details of the disposition of these early plots are missing. And the appropriation of lands for support of education and other public purposes was a recognized concept in later American history.

The issuing of patents in fee simple to land promised under the general land dividend did not reach the extent planned by the company until the arrival of Governor George Yeardley in 1619. There seems to be adequate evidence to prove, as Bruce contended, that a few grants had been made prior to this time, even prior to 1617; but no record has been preserved in the Virginia Land Office. However, even if such grants were authorized, it is unlikely that the proper surveys were made for many of them.

As early as 1616 there were references by the company to send to Virginia a surveyor who could lay out the lands to be distributed to the adventurers. It is probable that a surveyor accompanied Captain Samuel Argall to the colony in 1617, but the first name on record in this position seems to be that of Richard Norwood who had previously engaged in surveying in the Somer Isles. There is little to indicate that much was done by Norwood. In 1621 William Claiborne accompanied Governor Francis Wyatt to Virginia, and the arrival of these two men actuated the granting of many tracts.

One of these grants by Governor Wyatt is the earliest extant form of the headright franchise. Dated January 26, 1621/22, it conveyed to Thomas Hothersall 200 acres of land at Blunt Point located in later Warwick County. The grant read as follows:

By the Governr and Capt: Generll: of Virginia

To all to whome these prsents shall come greeting in our Lord God Everlasting.

Know Yee that I sr Francis Wyatt Kt, Governr and Capt: Generall of Virginia, by vertue of the great charter of orders and lawes concluded on and dated at London in a generall quarter court the eighteenth day of November one thousand six hundred and eighteene by the treasurer Counseil and company of adventurers for the first southerne colony of Virginia, according to the authority graunted them from his Matie under his great seale, the said charter being directed to the Governr and Counseil of State here resident, and by the rules of justice, equity & reason, doe wth the approbation and consent of the same Counseil who are joyned in commission with mee, give and graunt unto Mr. Thomas Hothersall of Paspehay gent., and to his heires and assignes for ever, for his first generll: devident, to bee augumented and doubled by the said company to him and his said heires and assignes when hee or they shall once sufficiently have planted and peopled the same.

Two hundred acres of land scituate and being at Blunt Point, confining on the east the land of Cornelius May, on the south upon the great river, on the north upon the maine land and on the west runing towards a small creek one hundred rod (at sixteene foote and a half the rod);

Fifty acres whereof is his owne psonall right and fifty acres is the psonall right of Frances Hothersall his wife, the other hundred acres in consideration of his transportacon of twoe of his children out of England at his owne cost & charges, Viz: Richard Hothersall and Mary Hothersall,

To Have and to Hold the said twoe hundred acres of land with all and singular the apptennces, and with his due share of all mines & minneralls therein conteyned, and wth all rights and privileges of hunting, hawking and fowling and others within the prcincts and upon the borders of the said land, To the only pper use benifitt and behoofe of the said Thomas Hothersall, his heires and assignes for ever,

In as large and ample manner to all intents and purposes as is specified in the said great charter or by consequences may justly bee collected out of the same, or out of his Ma'ties letters patents whereon it is grounded.

Yeilding and paying to the treasurer and company and to their successors for ever, yearely at the feast of St. Michael the Archangell [September 29], for every fifty acres, the fee rent of one shilling.

In witness whereof I have to these presents sett my hand and the great seale of the colony, given at James Citty the six and twentieth day of January one thousand six hundred twenty one [o.s.] and in the yeares of the raigne, of our Soveraigne Lord, James by the Grace of God King of England, Scotland, France and Ireland, Defender of the faith &c., Vizt: of England, France and Ireland the nineteenth and of Scotland the five and fiftieth, and in the fifteenth yeare of this plantacon.

Claiborne supervised most of the surveys included on the list of patents that was drawn up by Governor Wyatt in 1625. Out of 184 patents that were issued to individual planters, over seventy-five per cent included only 200 acres or less with the most frequent grant being the 100-acre grant to the "ancient planter." For the remaining individual grants, approximately one-sixth were between 201 and 600 acres; four were between 601 and 1,000 acres; and four exceeded 1,000 acres.

In an analysis of the status of the Virginia population with regard to landholding at the time of the dissolution of the company in 1624, Professor Manning C. Voorhis concluded that only about one-seventh of the 1,240 population obtained land from the company. This would leave the remainder of the settlers as indentured servants or tenant farmers who worked out their maintenance or transportation either for the company or for private individuals who financed their trip to America. The tenant farmers constituted the larger group. In the chapter that follows, some attention will be given to the status of these immigrants and the extent to which they were able to become independent landowners in the colony.

CHAPTER THREE
Virginia as a Royal Colony
The Nature and Size of Land Grants

A variety of reasons led the King to dissolve the London Company and to assume royal control over the first experiment in colonization under an incorporated company. Failure of the colony to thrive economically, the poor financial condition of the company, political differences between Sir Edwin Sandys and the King, internal dissensions between the Sandys faction and the Smith-Warwick group, the extremely high death rate in the colony, and the impact of the Indian massacre of 1622 — all contributed in varying degrees of importance to the dissolution. The company rejected efforts of the crown to substitute a new charter drawn up in 1623 providing for the King to resume control of the colony by establishing a royal Council in England and a Governor and Council in Virginia. Consequently the Privy Council obtained a writ of *quo warranto* which terminated with a decision by the court of King's Bench in May, 1624, annulling the charter of the company.

With the advent of royal control there was a significant continuity in practice in the colony, and the political framework was little changed. The Governor and Council were then appointed by the King, but the House of Burgesses continued without major revision. In order to assure continued respect for public authority, a royal commission was dispatched to Governor Wyatt and an eleven-man Council empowering them to act "as fully and ampley as anie Governor and Councell resident there at anie tyme within the space of five yeares now last past." A similar commission was issued to Sir George Yeardley in 1626, and for the next sixteen years royal instructions to the Governors reflected a striking resemblance.

A similar continuity was evident in economic affairs as revealed in land policy. The London Company as a corporate body in charge of the colony terminated in 1624 after eighteen years, and the following year after the death of King James I the colony of Virginia by proclamation was made a part of the royal demesne. The landholder in Virginia became then in effect a freehold tenant of the King. The rights and property of the company were taken over by the crown, but recognition was made of the private property right of the planter and of individual claims of those who had invested in the company. Even land rights to planters and adventurers that had not been taken up were recognized, but few proceeded to effect settlement or to exercise the right of taking up 100 acres per share of stock.

The land rights of the private joint-stock associations also continued to be recognized, but there was less enthusiasm on the part of individual adventurers to promote the projects started some years earlier. This development was indicative of the major change in the economic life of the colony that resulted in the decline, if not disappearance, of absentee ownership. As previously noted, Berkeley Hundred had suffered the loss of many of its settlers in the massacre of 1622; and upon expiration of term of service of the few remaining servants, only the land and a few cattle were left in the settlement. By 1636 the adventurers had sold their claims to London merchants. In the case of Martin's Hundred located about seven miles from Jamestown, the massacre doomed the active settlement and only the title to the land continued. Eventually the title to this hundred was withdrawn to permit natural expansion of the colony, and the associates or adventurers were awarded claims to land allotments commensurate with the number of shares held in the joint stock.

The tracts known as company land were maintained for a while under royal control. The role of the public estate, however, never assumed great significance, yet there is evidence of the continued practice during the seventeenth century of endowing an office such as Governor or secretary with the proceeds of a land grant.

Theoretically tenants and contract laborers who were still alive at the time of the dissolution of the company were to continue their labor either on the public land or on private associations. In practice, however, it is likely that lax enforcement of the contracts resulted in a substantial diminution of the obligations of many workers. The scarcity of records for this period makes it impossible to trace all of this group, but there is enough evidence to indicate that some continued to serve out their term of labor. The General Court in 1627 expressed concern about the approaching expiration of leases and indentures of persons for whom there were no provisions for lands; and action was taken to permit them to lease land for a period of ten to twenty-one years in return for which they were to render a stipulated amount of tobacco or corn for each acre, usually one pound of tobacco per acre. This lenient provision notwithstanding, only about sixty persons availed themselves of the opportunity, the remainder presumably either squatting on frontier land, working as laborers, or eventually obtaining title to land by purchase from an original patentee.

With the dissolution of the company the issuing of land patents continued in the hands of the Governor and Council. The King and Privy Council assumed power over land distribution but apparently left the issuing of patents as it had been before. Up until January, 1625, Governor Wyatt issued patents in the name of the company. At that time news reached Virginia that the writ of *quo warranto* of June, 1624, had dissolved the company and that King James I upon assumption of control of the colony had issued on August 26, 1624, the first commission of a royal Governor to Wyatt. But the commission made no reference to land grants, and Governor Wyatt issued none after January, 1625.

Charles I succeeded to the throne following the death of James I on March 27, 1625. His proclamation stating policy relative to Virginia professed protection of the interests of private planters and adventurers but made no direct reference to land grants. Governor Yeardley replaced Wyatt by a commission of March 14, 1625/26 and arrived in Virginia in May, 1626. There is no record extant to show that Yeardley received direct instructions to start issuing grants; but it is certain that he did begin in February, 1626/27, interpreting his instructions and commission as authorizing the action.

Land patents during this period were to be issued on four main conditions: (1) as a dividend in return for investment in the founding of the colony; (2) as a reward for special service to the colony; (3) as a stimulus to fortify the frontier by using land to induce settlement; and (4) as a method of encouraging immigration by the headright.

The first of these was simply an assurance by the King that the former stockholders in the company still had the right to take up land at the rate of 100 acres for each share of stock owned. As late as

1642 this privilege was still being confirmed in instructions to the Governor; but the stockholders appeared to be little interested at this time in coming to Virginia, for very few took up their claim and apparently the shares bearing the holder's name could not be transferred after the dissolution. The plan for the distribution of the first dividend in 1619 also provided for a second allotment. As late as 1632 patents still included authorization for a second dividend when the first had been cultivated. But no second allotment was ever made. There are, however, examples to indicate that claims for the first dividend were upheld after the company was dissolved. In 1628 Thomas Graies obtained a patent as a dividend for his subscription of twenty-five pounds sterling; in 1636 Captain John Hobson was issued a patent covering a bill of adventure that went back to 1621; and on another occasion the land dividend due a deceased father was awarded to his son.

The next condition of awarding patents for meritorious service to the colony was of long standing. Used to award ministers, political officials, physicians, sea captains, and various other individuals under the company, the practice continued under royal control after 1624. Governor Wyatt in 1638 was instructed to issue land patents for meritorious service according to provisions previously adopted for such cases. And a few years later Charles II awarded lands in Virginia to servants or others who aided him, although it is not certain whether these individuals were ever able to take up the claim bestowed upon them.

The third condition for a patent was practically a corollary to the second, for it involved rendering service to the colony by settling and fortifying the frontier. One example during this period may be found in securing the Peninsula. Following the massacre of 1622 Governor Wyatt and his Council wrote to the Earl of Southampton about a plan for "winning the forest" by running a pale between Martin's Hundred on the James River and Cheskiack on the York. Again in 1624 the suggestion was made to the royal commissioners who were sent over by the King to determine the most suitable places for fortification. To effect the construction of this palisade, the General Assembly in 1633 offered land as an inducement to settle between Queen's Creek and Archer's Hope Creek, promising fifty acres and a period of tax exemption to freemen who would occupy the area of Middle Plantation, later Williamsburg. In February, 1633, the order was issued for a fortieth part of the men in the "compasse of the forest" between the two previously mentioned creeks and Chesapeake Bay to meet at Dr. John Pott's plantation at the head of Archer's Hope Creek for the purpose of erecting houses to secure the neck of land known as the Peninsula. With this encouragement by the Assembly, a palisade six miles in length was completed, running from Queen's Creek to Archer's Hope Creek and passing through Middle Plantation. Houses were constructed at convenient distances, and a sufficient number of men were assigned to patrol the line of defense during times of imminent danger. By setting off a little less than 300,000 acres of land, this palisade provided defense for the new plantations between the York and James rivers and served as a restraining barrier for the cattle of the colony.

Granting of land was again used on a large scale for the establishment of forts after the Indian massacre of 1644. By order of the Assembly in 1645 blockhouses or forts were established at strategic points: Fort Charles at the falls of the James River, Fort Royal at Pamunkey, Fort James on the ridge of Chickahominy on the north side of the James, and in the next year Fort Henry at the falls of the Appomattox River. The maintenance of these forts involved considerable expense, more than the officials of the colony wished to drain from the public treasury. Therefore, they decided to grant the forts with adjoining lands to individuals who would accept the responsibility of their upkeep as well as the maintenance of an adequate force for defense. Fort Henry, located at present-day Petersburg, was granted to Captain Abraham Wood with 600 acres of land plus all houses, edifices, boats, and ammunition belonging to the fort. Wood was required to maintain and keep ten persons continuously at the fort for three years. During this time he was exempted from all public taxes for himself and the ten persons. Upon similar terms Lieutenant Thomas Rolfe, son of Pocahontas and John Rolfe, received Fort James and 400 acres of land; Captain Roger Marshall, Fort Royal and 600 acres. Since there was no arable land adjoining Fort Charles at present-day Richmond, other inducements were made for its maintenance. These forts served as the first line of defense against possible attacks by the natives. Being the center of the varied activities of the frontier, they also were the starting point for expeditions against the Indians and became the center of trade for the outlying regions.

The fourth condition for granting of land — the headright — was by far the most important and became the principal basis for title to land in the seventeenth century. Its origin goes back to "the greate charter" of 1618 in which the following provision was included:

That for all persons ... which during the next seven years after Midsummer Day 1618 shall go into Virginia with intent there to inhabite If they continue there three years or dye after they are shiped there shall be a grant made of fifty acres for every person upon a first division and as many more upon a second division (the first being peopled) which grants to be made respectively to such persons and their heirs at whose charges the said persons going to inhabite in Virginia shall be transported with reservation of twelve pence yearly rent for every fifty acres to be answered to the said treasurer and company and their successors for ever after the first seven years of every such grant.

Under these provisions of "the greate charter," it is evident that not only was the headright grant of fifty acres per person open to shareholders who brought settlers to the colony, but also to anyone who had migrated to the colony at his own expense or who had financed the expedition of other persons. Individuals paying their own transportation were entitled to fifty acres for themselves and for every member of the family, providing they fulfilled the residence requirement of three years.

Governors under the company issued patents based on the headright until dissolution by the crown in 1624. Beyond that time the status of the headright was uncertain. The "charter" of 1618 had specified a term for this right for seven years ending on Midsummer Day of 1625. After this term expired, royal governors continued to honor headright claims based on immigration, although no direct authorization for such action had come from the crown. Therefore, the issuance of these claims after 1625 was based primarily on custom, brief as it was, until more direct instructions were issued to Governor John Harvey in 1634 following the proprietary grant of Maryland in 1632.

The Maryland grant enhanced the concern of the Virginia inhabitants about their title to land, and correspondence conducted by Governor Harvey finally brought forth a statement from the Privy Council. Apprehension over Maryland led to assurance of the headright for Virginia as the Privy Council issued the following dispatch of July 22, 1634, to the Governor:

We have thought fit to certify you that his Majesty of his royal favor, and for the better encouragement of the planters there doth let you knowe that it is not intended that the interestes which men had settled when you were a corporation should be impeached; that for the present they may enjoy their estates and trades with the same freedom and privileges as they did before the recalling of their patents: To which purpose also in pursuance of his Majesty's gracious intention, wee doe hereby authorize you to dispose of such proportions of lands to all those planters beeing freemen as you had power to doe before the yeare 1625.

With this explicit royal endorsement of land patent principles followed under the company and confirmation of the headright, Governor Harvey modified the wording in the patents and adopted the following form illustrated in a grant of 2,500 acres to Captain Hugh Bullocke:

To all to whome these prsents. shall come, I Sr. John Harvey Kt. Governr. and Capt. Generll. of Virginia send greeting in our Lord God Everlasting.

Whereas by letters pattents bearing date the twoe and twentieth of July one thousand six hundred thirtie fower from the Rt. Honble. the Lords of his Majties. most Honoble. Privie Councell their lordshipps did authorize the Governr. and Councell of Virginia to dispose of such pportions of land to all planters being freemen as they had power to doe before the yeare 1625, whene according to divers orders & constitutions in that case provided and appointed all devidents of lands any waies due or belonging to any adventurers or planters of what condicon soever were to bee laid out and assigned unto them according to the severall condicons in the same menconed.

Now Know Yee therefore that I the said Sr. John Harvey doe, with the consent of the Councell of State give and graunt unto Capt.

Hugh Bullocke and to his heires and assignes for ever by these prsents

Twoe thousand five hundred and fiftie acres of land, scituate, lying & being from the runn that falleth downe by the eastern side of a peece of land knowne by the name of the Woodyard and soe from that runn along the side of the Pocoson (or great Otter pond soe called) northwest and about the head of the said Otter pond back southeast leaveing the Otter pond in the middle.

To have and to Hold the said twoe thousand five hundred and fiftie acres of land with his due share of all mines and minneralls therein conteyned and with all rights and priviledges of hunting, hawking, fishing and fowling, wth in the prcincts of the same to the sole and pper use benifitt and behoofe of him the said Capt. Bullocke his heires and assignes for ever.

In as large and ample manner to all intents and purposes as is expressed in the said orders and constitutions, or by consequence may bee justly collected out of the same or out of his Majties. letters pattents whereon they are grounded.

Yielding and paying for every fiftie acres of land herein by these presents given and graunted yearely at the feast of St. Michaell the Archangell [September 29], the fee rent of one shilling to his Majties. use.

Provided always that [if] the said Capt. Hugh Bullock, his heires or assignes shall not plant or seate or cause to bee planted on the said twoe thousand five hundred & fiftie acres of land wth in the time and terms of three yeares now next ensuing the date hereof, that then it shall and may bee lawfull for any adventurer or planter to make choice and seate upon the same.

Given at James Citty under my hand and sealed with the seale of the colony the twelfth day of March one thousand six hundred thirtie fower [o.s.] & in the tenth year of our Soveraigne Lord King Charles &c.

Use of the headright had been adopted by the company as an expedient to increase population of the colony and to encourage immigration without further expenditure from the company treasury. The practice continued with the fifty acres of land granted to the persons who financed the transportation of the immigrant, but the grant itself was not valuable enough to compensate for the expense involved. Therefore, with increasing frequency the system of indentured servitude was used whereby the immigrant agreed to an indenture or contract to work a certain number of years as additional payment for his transportation. This system, in general, proved advantageous to both the master and the servant, to the colony by providing additional immigrants, and to England by serving as a vent for surplus population.

Indentured servants were not slaves but were servants during the specified period of the contract. While the laws of the time did make a distinction in the severity of the penal code as applied to servants and to freemen, still indentured servitude did not have the stigma of bondage or slavery; and many servants upon completion of their term of service rose to positions of social and political prominence in the history of the colony. In 1676 the Lords of Trade and Plantations expressed concern over the use of the word "servitude" because of the implications of slavery, and they preferred "to use the word service, since those servants are only apprentices for years."

At the expiration of the term of service, the servants usually received equipment and supplies necessary to start them as freemen. They received grain enough for one year, clothes, and in some cases a gun and a supply of tools. As to receipt of land, the policy varied from one colony to another, and at times there was uncertainty within one colony about obligations to freedmen. In Virginia the indentured servant did not usually receive land at the end of service unless he had insisted, as John Hammond in *Leah and Rachel* had advised, that a specific provision be included in the contract to include the award of fifty acres as "freedom's dues." There are some cases in which the provision for land was included as illustrated in one of the earliest indentures known to exist for Virginia. This indenture of September 7, 1619, was made between Robert Coopy of North Nibley in Gloucestershire with the associates of Berkeley Hundred. Coopy agreed to work three years in Virginia and submit to the government of the hundred in return for which the owners were to transport him to Virginia and "There to maintayne him with convenient diet and apparell meet for such a servant, and in the end of the said terme to make him a free man of the said cuntry theirby to enjoy all the liberties, freedomes, and priviledges of a freeman there, and to grant to the said Robert thirty acres of land within their territory or hundred of Barkley...."

The confusion over the question whether the indentured servant was entitled to fifty acres of land upon expiration of his service extended to the mother country. There was a widespread belief in England that such was the case, and there were indefinite statements in commissions and instructions to the Governors that left the matter in doubt. In practice in Virginia, however, it is certain that the fifty acres under the headright claim went to the person transporting indentured servants, not to the servants themselves. Only where the contract specifically stated that the servant was to receive fifty acres was he assured of this grant.

Under the company there had been definite provisions that the fifty acres went to the persons transporting servants, not to the servants themselves. After its dissolution, Governors were instructed to follow the rules of the "late company," and this continued until there was a variation in Sir Francis Wyatt's commission of 1639 authorizing the Governor and the Council to issue grants to adventurers and planters "According to the orders of the late company ... and likewise 50 acres of land to every person transported thither ... until otherwise determined by His Majesty." Did "to every person" mean that the servant was entitled to land? Such was the case across the Potomac in Maryland where the servant could claim fifty acres from his employer or master until 1646; after 1646 and until 1683 the proprietor provided land for the servant. If such were intended, it was not followed and the intentions were far from clear in the later commission to Sir William Berkeley in 1642. In addition to assigning land for "adventurers of money" and "transportation of people," the commission authorized the Governor and Council to grant "fifty acres for every person transported thither since Midsummer 1625, and ... continue the same course to all persons transported thither until it shall otherwise be determined by His Majesty." The loose use of the terminology "to" and "for" recurred in subsequent years and again reflected the lack of precision in this matter as well as the seeming misapprehension in England that the servant was entitled to a fifty-acre grant. Under the articles of the treaty of 1651 between Virginia and the commissioners of the Commonwealth, the reversion to the term "for every person" was made and the policy of no land to servants was implicit in the sixth article of the agreement: "That the priviledge of haveing fiftie acres of land for every person transported in the collony shall continue as formerly granted."

Even though servants were not granted land by the colony at the expiration of their service, a substantial number soon became land-owners. The exact proportion of servants that became landholders after 1624 cannot be determined in the absence of a complete census. However, an examination of the land patents and the list of headrights makes possible some estimate of the percentage of land-holders that had once been indentured servants. The conclusions cannot be final and are subject to limitations. Identification presents a problem because of the frequency of the same name as Smith or Davis and because of the omission of middle names. The problem is further complicated by the fact that headrights were often trans-ferred by sale. A person entitled to a headright claim on the frontier may not have wished to settle there; rather he may have preferred to sell his headright claim and purchase land in an established county. As a result of the sale of his headright claim, his name may have appeared in the headright list as the basis for the claim for someone else even though he had not been an indentured servant. Therefore, all persons so listed under the headright claim cannot be considered indentured servants.

Fully aware of the limitations just suggested and equally con-scious that estimates in the absence of more complete records can-not be final, Professor Thomas J. Wertenbaker in his *Planters of Colo-nial Virginia* summarized his analysis of patents and concluded that both before 1635 and in the following two or three decades, thirty to forty per cent of the landholders of Virginia came to the colony as indentured servants.

Professor Wertenbaker also indicated general agreement with conclusions drawn by William G. Stanard about the proportion of immigrants that were indentured servants. From an analysis of the patent rolls from 1623 to July 14, 1637, printed in the April, 1901, issue of the *Virginia Magazine of History and Biography*, Stanard esti-mated that seventy-five per cent of immigrants from 1623 to 1637 were imported under term of the indenture. Out of 2,675 names on the rolls, 336 entered as freemen at their own cost and an additional 245 persons were believed for the most part to be of the same status although there was some uncertainty about this group. Transportation expenses were paid by others for 2,094. From these numbers, the conclusion was reached that 675 persons on the patent rolls were freemen, including women and children; the remaining 2,000 were servants and slaves, the latter in very small number at this time. Thus the analysis roughly confirms the conclusion that three-fourths of the immigrants during this period were indentured servants.

Use of the headright system for distribution of land had a close correlation with expanding population, for it was hoped that the increase of population would keep pace with the acquisition of private title in the soil. As the seventeenth century progressed, there were many abuses and evasions of the system; and by the end of the period its significance declined in favor of acquisition of title by purchase, or the "treasury right." To understand the various deviations from the system, it will be helpful to review the steps by which title to land by headright was obtained.

The first step involved the proving of the headright by the claimant appearing before either a county court or the Governor and Council and stating under oath that he had imported a certain number of persons whose names were listed. The clerk of the court issued a certificate which was validated in the secretary's office. Authorization for the headright was then passed on to a commissioned surveyor who ran off fifty acres for each person imported and located the grant in the area selected by the claimant as long as the land had not already been patented and had not been barred for white settlement in order to maintain peace with the Indians. Upon completion of the survey and of marking the boundaries, a copy of the record along with the headright certificate was presented to the secretary's office where a patent was prepared and a notation made of those imported. The final step was the signing of the patent by the Governor in the presence of, and with the approval of, the Council.

One deviation from the spirit of the law of the headright involved claims based upon the person being imported into the colony more than once. For example, John Chew in 1637 received 700 acres, using his own transportation in 1622 and 1623 as the basis for the claim to 100 acres in the grant. Carrying this practice to a greater extreme, Sarah Law received a grant for 300 acres of land based upon the fact that she had imported John Good, probably a sailor, six times.

On a larger scale, ship masters submitted lists for headright claims which in actuality contained the roster of both the sailors of the ship and the passengers. In neither case should the right have been acknowledged, for the sailors were under agreement to continue service at sea and the passengers had paid their own transportation to the colony. But the lax administration of the system usually permitted approval of such applications, and the ship master therefore found himself with headright certificates which he could sell to others for whatever price he could wangle. This practice was sometimes repeated by the same unscrupulous ship master who was aided in the irregular procedure by the failure of the clerks of the secretary's office to make careful checks of lists submitted, and also by the fact that he could present his lists to a different county court when importing the same sailors for the third or fourth time.

Like the ship master, the sailor engaged in falsifying the record by swearing that he had imported himself and sometimes others at his own expense. Patents were obtained on the basis of the headright. Philip A. Bruce concluded that the land obtained in Virginia by mariners was "very extensive." To substantiate this general statement, he referred to powers of attorney found in the county court records, authorizing an agent in Virginia to handle the estates of the mariner. In the records of Rappahannock County for 1668 is an example of the practice, in which Thomas Sheppard of Plymouth, England, designated William Moseley to handle his interest in 150 headrights which he claimed for importing 150 people to Virginia. It was likely in this case that duplicate claims were issued, either to the individual if he paid his own transportation or to some master if the immigrant became an indentured servant. In some instances, as many as three or four claims were made for one importation: one for the ship master, one for the merchant who acted as middle-man in purchasing the service of the immigrant, one for the planter who eventually purchased the indentured servant, and less often one for a second planter who may have joined with the first in obtaining the services of the imported person.

As abuse of the system increased, headright lists sometimes included fictitious names or in some cases names copied from old record books. The final stage in irregular procedure was reached when the clerks in the office of the secretary of the colony sold the headright claim to persons who would simply pay from one to five shillings. The exact date at which this practice began has not been determined, but it was prevalent sometime before 1692. Francis Nicholson reported to the Board of Trade that while serving as Governor of Virginia from 1690 to 1692, he had "heard" that the sale of rights by the clerks in the secretary's office was "common practice." Another report to the Board in 1697 described the clerks as being "a constant mint of those rights."

The combined variations in the operation of the headright system resulted in the distortion, if not destruction, of its original concepts. The system continued to bring immigrants into the colony which had been a very important purpose when inaugurated. But the abuses threw out of balance the relation between patented land and the number of people in the colony; and furthermore through perversion of the system, speculation in land was not prevented and there resulted large areas of wholly uncultivated and uninhabited lands to which title had been granted. The headright was also originally intended to apply to inhabitants of the British Isles, but by the middle of the seventeenth century the names of persons imported from Africa appeared occasionally as the basis for headright, and by the last decade of the century they were frequently found.

The distortion of the headright system was done with considerable public approval and in some ways reflected the evolution of economic development that seemed to demand a more convenient and less expensive method for obtaining title to large areas of unoccupied land. As the population of the colony increased and as the labor supply became more plentiful, there was a rather widespread demand to be able to obtain additional land, particularly adjacent undeveloped tracts, without having to import an additional person for every fifty acres. Partly through this demand, impetus was given to the custom, which was not at first sanctioned by law, to permit the granting of patents by simply paying a fee in the secretary's office.

While the headright system was designed to maintain some proportion between the population of the colony and the amount of land patented, it was also designed to stimulate the migration of immigrants to the colony. Therefore, under the system it was possible for individuals who would engage in transporting or financing the transportation of immigrants to obtain large areas of land. This trend was started under the company; and in the four years prior to 1623, forty-four patents of 5,000 acres each were awarded to persons who were to transport at least 100 immigrants to the colony. In 1621, for example, 5,000 acres were granted to Arthur Swain and Nathaniel Basse and a similar grant to Rowland Truelove and "divers other patentees" each grant to be based on the transportation of 100 persons; 15,000 acres were to go to Sir George Yeardley for engaging to transport 300 persons.

For the years following the dissolution of the company, valuable information of the nature and size of land grants can be found in the "Virginia Land Patents" which fortunately have survived the usual hazards of fire and carelessness. The two following tables (Tables I and II) have been compiled from the analysis of the land patents by Philip A. Bruce and summarized in his *Economic History of Virginia* (volume I, pages 528-532).

I. Table Showing Size of Land Grants From 1626 to 1650
Based on the Record of Virginia Land Patents

Year or years	Average grant for the period	Largest grant for the period
1626-1632	100-300 acres	1,000 acres
1634	719 acres	5,350 acres
1635	380 acres	2,000 acres
1636	351 acres	2,000 acres
1637	445 acres	5,350 acres
1638	423 acres	3,000 acres
1640	405 acres	1,300 acres
1641	343 acres	872 acres

1642	559 acres	3,000 acres
1643	595 acres	4,000 acres
1644	370 acres	670 acres
1645	333 acres	1,090 acres
1646	360 acres	1,200 acres
1647	361 acres	650 acres
1648	412 acres	1,800 acres
1649	522 acres	3,500 acres
1650	677 acres	5,350 acres

II. Table Showing Size of Land Grants From 1650 to 1700
Based on the Record of Virginia Land Patents

Period of years	Average grant for the period	Number of largest grants for the period	
1650-1655	591 acres	1,000 - 2,000 acres	(92)
		2,000 - 5,000 acres	(41)
		5,000 - 10,000 acres	(3)
1655-1666	671 acres	1,000 - 2,000 acres	(252)
		2,000 - 5,000 acres	(147)
		5,000 - 10,000 acres	(20)
1666-1679	890 acres	1,000 - 2,000 acres	(220)
		2,000 - 5,000 acres	(154)
		5,000 - 10,000 acres	(25)
		10,000 - 20,000 acres	(12)
1679-1689	607 acres	1,000 - 2,000 acres	(143)
		2,000 - 5,000 acres	(66)
		5,000 - 10,000 acres	(17)
		10,000 - 20,000 acres	(2)
1689-1695	601 acres	1,000 - 2,000 acres	(63)
		2,000 - 5,000 acres	(23)
		5,000 - 10,000 acres	(7)

1695-1700	688 acres	1,000 - 2,000 acres	(14)
		2,000 - 5,000 acres	(13)
		5,000 - 10,000 acres	(7)
		13,400 acres	(1)

[Note: In compiling this table, two changes have been made to correct what seems clearly to be errors in Bruce's description. Forty-one grants were listed for 2,000-5,000 acres from 1650-1655 rather than forty-one grants of 1,000-5,000 acres as noted by Bruce. The date 1685 listed in Bruce has been changed to 1689 to give the proper time period of 1689-1695.]

For the period from 1634 to 1650 included in Table I, there were occasional grants of 5,000 acres, but the average size of the patents for the period was not over 446 acres. It was possible, of course, for one individual to build up a large landed estate by putting together several smaller grants; and this was done by a limited number of persons during the seventeenth century in Virginia as will be discussed later. There was also the possibility that grants of considerable size in the original patent might be broken up and distributed to others in smaller amounts. In any case, the second half of the century as reflected in the land patents saw a moderate increase in the size and number of large grants as the population increased, and the average size for the land patent of this period was 674 acres, an increase of 228 acres over the period prior to 1650.

While the second half of the century witnessed this increase, much of it came during the third quarter of the period. Near the end of the century there was a definite trend to break up some of the larger patents into smaller landholdings by sales to servants completing their indenture, by distribution of land to children, or by sale because of an inadequate labor supply either of slaves, indentured servants, tenant farmers, or wage earners.

The existence of the small farm and the small farmer as a major part of the socio-economic system of Virginia at the end of the seventeenth century has been well established. Professor Wertenbaker suggested that "a full 90 per cent of the freeholders" at the time the rent roll was compiled in 1704/05 included the "sturdy, independent class of small farmers." Through examination of land patents, land transfers, tax rolls, and a sampling of other county records, he found substantial evidence to corroborate the suggested trend of the breakup of a number of large patents and their distribution to small freeholders. Illustrative of this development was the land known as Button's Ridge in Essex County. Originally including 3,650 acres, the tract was patented to Thomas Button in 1666. The estate then passed first to the brother of Button and later was sold to John Baker. Baker divided the large tract and sold small amounts to the following people: 200 acres to Captain William Moseley, 600 to John Garnet, 200 to Robert Foster, 200 to William Smither, 200 to William Howlett, 300 to Anthony Samuell, and 200 to William Williams.

Professor Susie M. Ames in *Studies of the Virginia Eastern Shore in the Seventeenth Century* found evidence of the same trend by which original land grants increased in size by the middle of the century and reached its peak in the third quarter of the century. Near the end of the period many of the larger tracts were being divided by wills distributing them among children or by sales in smaller units. Much of the land obtained by the first two generations on the Eastern Shore was broken up into small holdings by the third. As stated by Professor Ames, "It is the subtraction and division of acres, with only occasionally any marked addition, that seems to be the chief development in land tenure during the last quarter of the seventeenth century."

Even with the trend of dividing some of the large estates on the Eastern Shore, a small per cent of the population held a considerable part of the land. In 1703/04 the average size of landholding in Northampton County was 389 acres, in Accomack 520 acres. When analyzed by use of the list of tithables, Northampton County had twenty-one persons, only three per cent of the tithables, holding thirty-nine per cent of the land; Accomack County had a total of forty-six persons, only four per cent of the tithables, holding forty-three per cent of the land.

Considering all of Virginia of the seventeenth century, one cannot say that it was primarily a land of large plantations, of cavaliers, and of noble manors which have been romanticized by some writers. Yet there was a significant number of prominent planters who took an active part in the social and political life of the colony and exerted an influence disproportionate to their ratio of the population. Professor Wertenbaker listed the following men among the prominent planters of the first half of seventeenth-century Virginia—George Menefie, Richard Bennett, and Richard Kinsman; for the second half of the century, a more extensive list—Nathaniel Bacon, Sr., Thomas Ballard, Robert Beverley, Giles Brent, Joseph Bridger, William Byrd I, John Carter, John Custis I, Dudley Digges, William Fitzhugh, Lewis Burwell, Philip Ludwell I, William Moseley, Daniel Parke, Ralph Wormeley, Benjamin Harrison, Edward Hill, Edmund Jennings, and Matthew Page. Members of this group accumulated large landholdings, mostly by original patent through the headright system or by private purchase from holders of original patents. For example, William Byrd I had obtained 26,231 acres of land at the time of his death; and William Fitzhugh acquired during his lifetime 96,000 acres of land and left at the time of his death in 1701 a little over 54,000 acres in family "seats" to five sons.

The land system and its administration that permitted the accumulation of a few of these substantial plantations came under detailed discussion by crown officials near the end of the seventeenth century. Before examining this analysis of Virginia land policy, it will be helpful to survey in the following chapter the major laws and the officials responsible for their administration.

CHAPTER FOUR
Royal Administration of Land Policy
Attempts at Reform

The issuing of land patents and the administration of laws concerning land involved a variety of officials during the seventeenth century. Under the company the authority to convey title to land rested after 1609 with the treasurer, the Council in London, and the association of adventurers in England. The Governor and Council in the colony were authorized as ministerial agents of the company to make grants, but final approval was to be made at sessions of the quarter court of the company in England. This last step, as previously noted, was seldom completed. After dissolution of the company, the process of issuing patents was simplified. Most grants were made under the headright claim and followed the steps outlined in chapter three, involving the county court, the secretary of the colony, the Governor and Council, and the commissioned surveyors.

The office of surveyor existed under the company and William Claiborne, who came to the colony in 1621, was the first to fill the position effectively. As surveyor, Claiborne received the annual wage of thirty pounds sterling which was to be paid either in tobacco or some other comparable commodity with a good price on the English market. Surveyor Claiborne also had the use of a house constructed by the company as well as receiving the necessary equipment and books needed for his work.

Following the dissolution of the company in 1624, the office of surveyor-general was established with a royal appointee who was charged with the responsibility of maintaining the survey records and issuing commissions to the surveyors of the colony. Some difficulty was encountered in securing qualified and reliable men. This led during the interregnum to a law in March, 1654/55, calling for the dismissal of unqualified surveyors and placing the power of appointment in the hands of the county court. After the restoration of Charles II to the throne, the appointment of surveyors returned to the system of commissions from the surveyor-general.

The amount for surveyors' fees was designated by the legislature at various times. Ten pounds of tobacco for every 100 acres was specified in 1624; in 1642 and again in 1646 the fee limit was raised to twenty pounds of tobacco for measuring 100 acres of land with an additional allowance of twelve pounds of tobacco for each day that the task required the surveyor to be away from his home. If his transportation could be only by water, the person employing him was required to assume the expense of travel both to and from the location of the survey. In 1661/62 the allowance for each day away from home was increased to thirty pounds of tobacco; and by the same law the surveyor was authorized the same limit of twenty pounds of tobacco for running off 100 acres if the total was greater than 500, otherwise he was to receive a minimum of 100 pounds of tobacco. Efforts to obtain capable, honest, and conscientious appointees continued to be a problem. The need for better surveyors and the decline of the tobacco prices led the Assembly to double the previous fees. In 1666 forty pounds of tobacco was stipulated for surveying 100 acres if the total was for 1,000 acres. If less than 1,000, the allowance was 400 pounds of tobacco.

Commissioned surveyors were not at liberty to refuse reasonable requests for surveys to be made, except in cases involving sickness or some other impediment recognized as legal. The law of 1666 provided that anyone violating this requirement was subject to a fine of 4,000 pounds of tobacco; for charging excessive fees, the fine was 200 pounds of tobacco that could be recovered in the Virginia courts.

Gabriel Hawley, Robert Evelyn, Thomas Loving, Edmund Scarborough, and Alexander Culpeper served as surveyor-general with the last named having Philip Ludwell as his deputy. Upon the chartering of the College of William and Mary surveyors were appointed by the institution, and the appointees were required to contribute to the trustees of the college one-sixth of the fees of the office. The trustees were permitted to delegate the appointments. Consequently in 1692 they designated Miles Cary as surveyor-general, who was instructed to make the selection of surveyors with the aid of a committee named by the trustees.

In addition to the fees of the surveyor, there were other charges that were made from time to time in obtaining a patent in Virginia. Under the company without a legal guide for the fees to be charged, the secretary of the colony apparently demanded at times as much as twenty pounds of tobacco or three pounds sterling when issuing a title for the individual dividends of fifty or 100 acres. Leaders of the company considered this fee unreasonable and took steps to prevent its collection.

Following the dissolution of the company, the Assembly set the fees of the secretary regarding land patents along with other authorized charges. In 1632 the secretary collected thirty pounds of tobacco for issuing a patent plus two pounds for each sheet required to record the document. In 1633 the fee for patents by the secretary was designated as fifteen shillings which could be collected either in tobacco or corn according to current price. Ten years later in 1643 the fee for a patent was again listed in terms of tobacco at fifty pounds with six pounds allowed for each recorded sheet. In lieu of four pounds of tobacco, the secretary was authorized to receive money at the rate of twelve pence for every four pounds of tobacco. At the March session of the legislature in 1657/58, the secretary's fees were further raised to eighty pounds of tobacco for issuing and recording a patent; thirty pounds was set as the fee for supplying a copy of the patent later; and fifteen pounds of tobacco was authorized for providing a certificate for land. These same fees of 1657/58 were repeated by law in 1661/62.

The stamp of the seal of the colony was required during much of the seventeenth century as the final step of approval for a patent, and during most of the time no fee was charged for this. However, under the governorship of Lord Howard which began in April, 1684, a charge of 200 pounds of tobacco was ordered for use of the seal for patents as well as all public documents such as commissions and proclamations. The proceeds from this fee were used by the Governor and were estimated by William Fitzhugh to equal 100,000 pounds of tobacco each year. However, such strong opposition was raised to the charge that it was dropped after 1689.

In addition to controversies over fees, there were many problems that arose in seventeenth-century Virginia over surveys and the identification of boundaries. Surveyors usually took the edge of a stream, either a river or creek, as the base line of the survey and then ran the boundaries for a specified distance along a line at right angle to the base. Terminal points were laid out and witnessed by neighboring owners with some distinguishing mark as a large stone or a tree with three or four chops. In 1679 a question was called to the attention of the Assembly as to the extent of the owner's rights along the water's edge. The case arose over the complaint of Robert Liny that part of his patent along the river had been cleared for fishing but the exercise of his fishing rights had been hampered by trespassing individuals who dragged their seines upon the river's edge, claiming that "The water was the kings majesties ... and therefore equally free to all his majesties subjects to fish in and hale their sceanes on shore...." In answer to this complaint, the Assembly declared that the rights of the patent holder extended into the stream as far as the low water mark, and any person fishing or seining without permission within these bounds was guilty of trespass.

More frequently problems arose as a result of defective surveys either in the first line along the edge of the stream or in a second and third line of patents that were laid out when all land along the streams had been occupied. Some of the surveys were inaccurate because of the lack of graduation on the compass; others were distorted by careless surveyors selecting convenient terminal points such as a tree, a road, or another stream and ignoring the accurate measurement of the line. As early as 1623/24, the Assembly ordered that individual land dividends be surveyed and the bounds recorded; and in case serious disputes arose over conflicting boundaries, appeal could be made to the Governor and Council. In an effort to prevent the holder of patents from having to pay for more than one survey of the same grant, the Assembly in 1642/43 stated that surveys made by commissioned surveyors were considered valid and bestowed full right of ownership without the necessity and expense of new surveys. Such a provision did not, however, resolve the problem that arose over errors made by commissioned surveyors, errors that may have led a person in good faith to construct buildings on a plot that was later determined to be a part of the patent of his neighbor. Several cases having arisen over this situation, the Assembly in 1642/43 and again in 1657/58 and 1661/62 provided that when one person had unknowingly erected constructions on another person's land, the original owner as shown by survey was to have the right to purchase the improvements at a price fixed by a twelve-man jury. If the amount proved too great for the original owner, then the person seating the land by mistake was to have the option of purchasing the land at a price set by the jury for its value before seating occurred. Beginning with the 1657/58 statement of the law, no consideration was to be given if construction had been made after legal warning had been given to desist.

Other legislation was designed to minimize the number of cases of this type that would arise. One provision made in 1646 required the person claiming to be the original owner of the land to file suit against his encroaching neighbor within five years for removal; otherwise possession of the land for five years without contest would prevent recovery by the original claimant. The law exempted orphans from the above provision and permitted them a five-year period after coming of age. A later enactment in 1657/58 repeated the provision on orphans and added to the exemption married women and persons of unsound mind. A second provision designed to prevent quarrels among neighbors required a person holding patent to land adjacent to a proposed grant to show the boundaries of his property within twelve months; otherwise the latest grant as surveyed would be valid and would take precedence over the old patent.

But these various laws did not prevent "contentious suites" from arising because of defective surveys when the lines were first run or because the restriction against resurveys did not resolve the boundary disputes. Conflicts continued if the surveyor had been negligent in marking clearly the boundaries, or if lines had become indistinct by the chops in trees filling out, by piles of stones being scattered, or by trees being removed. To prevent "the inconvenience of clandestine surveigh," the Assembly in 1661/62 enacted the law of processioning. By this provision the members of each community were to "goe in procession" once every four years to examine and renew, if necessary, the boundary lines. Boundaries acknowledged by the procession as correct were conclusive and prohibited later claims to change them. If controversy arose over the line, the two surveyors accompanying the party were to run the line anew, disputes were to be equitably settled, and the line so laid out to be final. For administration of processioning, the county court was to order the vestry to divide each parish into as many precincts as necessary, and the time set in 1661/62 for processioning was between Easter and Whitsunday (seventh Sunday or fiftieth day after Easter). The time was changed in 1691 to the months from September to March as a more convenient period. To assure enforcement of the law, provisions for penalties were included—1,200 pounds of tobacco for any vestry not ordering the processioning and 350 pounds of tobacco for individuals who failed to participate without good reason.

Still other problems concerning land patents related to two important conditions stipulated for perfection of the title to land—the first, "seating and planting," and the second, the collection of a quit-rent. With the exception of some of the early grants, the patents of seventeenth-century Virginia required "seating and planting" of the tract within three years. As shown in the form used by Governor William Berkeley during the 1660's, if the patentee "His heirs or assignes doe not seate or plant or cause to be planted or seated on the sayd land within three years next ensueing, then it shall be lawful for any adventurer or planter to make choyse or seate thereupon." The time limit was extended as the exigency demanded. Because of losses from the Indian massacre of 1644, of the shortage of corn, and of the need for additional servants, the Assembly ruled that persons affected by the massacre were permitted three additional years to comply with the requirement for "seating and planting." Following the Indian disturbances of Bacon's Rebellion, the time period for plantations that were attacked was extended to seven years from the date the Assembly passed the act in 1676/77.

Generally speaking, however, the requirement for "seating and planting" was not carried out effectively, and there was little forfeiture because of noncompliance. In 1657/58 the Assembly recognized the right for patents to be issued on order of the Governor and Council for land "deserted for want of planting within the time of three yeeres." But even if such forfeiture did occur, the original patent holder was authorized to take up additional land elsewhere in the colony without complying with the headright requirement. And it was not until 1666 that the Assembly gave a definition for "seating and planting" in the declaration that "Building an house and keeping a stock one whole yeare upon the land shall be accounted seating; and that cleering, tending and planting an acre of ground shall be accounted planting." Either one or the other fulfilled the condition for the patent, and throughout the seventeenth century there was no relation between the size of the tract and the amount of improvement required. The minimum performance satisfied the law. Therefore, either the building of a small cabin, putting a few cattle or a few hogs on the tract for a year, or planting as little as an acre of ground — any one of the three protected the grant.

For most of the patents issued, this requirement presented little problem because the owner was interested in settling and improving his holdings. Violation of the provision was most likely to come in the case of land speculators who had taken up large tracts or in the case of landholders who were interested in acquiring adjacent tracts for the purpose of grazing or for forest supply. In the case of the latter, there was some question whether the requirement applied to adjacent tracts; but the Assembly in 1692 declared that tracts added to an original patent must be seated and planted as the law provided for other grants.

To a considerable extent there was the same attitude toward the requirement for "seating and planting" as has been noted previously for obtaining patent by headright. Light regard for the spirit of the law and at times the letter of the law came in part as a result of the unlimited expanse of land that tempted the established settler as well as the newcomer. Evasion of the law cast no stigma upon the offender, and some who were aware of their neighbor's dereliction winked at the action, thinking perhaps that they too might sometime engage in the same practice. Furthermore, the necessity of the provision for "seating and planting" which was well founded for the early years of the colony decreased in significance as the population and occupied areas of Virginia increased.

The second condition for perfection of title to land — payment of a quitrent — likewise had a checkered career in the seventeenth century. Under the company there is some question whether quitrents were due. It is clear that "the greate charter" of 1618 in order to encourage immigration exempted for seven years settlers who were taking up land by headright. For planters settled before 1616 at the expense of the company, it seems that they would have been free of paying the quitrent only for a seven-year period which would have required compliance before dissolution of the company. Settlers who arrived in Virginia after Dale's departure in 1616 and before 1618 would most probably have been subject to the quitrent under the company since they were exempt for only seven years. Whatever the case, there were rents to be collected before 1624 as shown by the duties of George Sandys, younger brother of Sir Edwin Sandys and first appointee to the office of treasurer in Virginia. Sandys was instructed to collect some £1,000 owed the company either as rent or as dues.

When Virginia became a royal colony in 1624, the quitrents were then payable at the rate of one shilling for every fifty acres patented. For 1631 the estimate was made by the Assembly that the quitrents would bring in as much as 2,000 pounds sterling, if paid. But little effort was being made to collect the rent and it was not until 1636 that Jerome Hawley was appointed treasurer. His arrival in the colony the following year initiated plans for collection. Proceeds from this source of revenue were to be used for the treasurer's salary; any surplus amount was to be used at the discretion of the Assembly. In order to determine who owed the rent, instructions were issued to landholders in Virginia to show their land titles to the treasurer in order that he could compute the rents that were due. But little action was taken and it seems certain that not enough was collected to pay the salary of the treasurer. In 1639 additional provisions were stipulated by the Assembly to tighten the quitrent collection by requiring landholders upon summon by warrant to reveal their title and the size of their estates to commissioners of the county courts. Following the precedent of "the greate charter" of 1618, no rents were to be paid until the expiration of seven years. This provision continued in effect under Charles I and during the interregnum, but the time limit was retracted in the instructions to Governor William Berkeley under Charles II. The retraction was confirmed under James II, the major reason being that it encouraged individuals to take up larger areas of land than they were able to cultivate.

Collection of quitrents, however, continued to lag and around 1646 no more than 500 pounds sterling was being collected. The treasurer appealed to the Assembly which acknowledged that "There is and hath been great neglect in the payment of the quitt rent." Consequently the Assembly in 1647 authorized the treasurer to levy a distress upon the property of delinquent taxpayers. The delinquent was permitted, if providing security, to retain his goods under replevin and to have a hearing before either a county court or the Governor and Council for final disposition of the case. Such a measure, however, was not effective against land not seated and planted, for the land itself was not to be seized; and a similar handicap prevailed against absentee owners as far as action by the treasurer was concerned.

Assistance in collection of quitrents was provided by the sheriff who was designated as the recipient of payments for each county with the fee of ten per cent of the collections being allowed him. Using the patent rolls of his office, both past and current, as a guide, the sheriff collected the rent and turned it over to the auditor of the colony. The rent was received either in coin or in tobacco as the law provided from time to time. In 1661, for example, persons unable to pay in coin were permitted by law to pay in tobacco at the rate of two pence per pound. But there was considerable controversy over the nature of the payment, and King James II ordered the repeal of the earlier act because of the poor quality of tobacco being submitted. After the overthrow of the King in 1688/89, the collection of quitrents continued for the most part in tobacco at the rate of one penny per pound.

In 1671 the privilege of collecting and using the quitrents was granted to Colonel Henry Norwood, who had supported faithfully the King and the royal cause during the civil war. Two years later the quitrents were given to Lords Arlington and Culpeper, including collections that might be made of rents in arrears. Protests from Virginia of these grants forced the revocation of the special gifts in 1684, although Culpeper retained the right to the quitrents in the Northern Neck.

Collection of quitrents at various times was farmed out to members of the Council and to the Governor, with the Councilor concerned usually taking the counties near his own residence. In 1665, for example, Governor William Berkeley assumed the collection in James City and Surry counties; Colonel Miles Cary, in Warwick and Elizabeth City counties; Nathaniel Bacon, Sr., for York County, the Isle of Wight, and the southern part of New Kent; and similar designations for other members of the Council. In 1699, however, the Council ordered William Byrd, auditor of the colony, to sell the quitrents of each county to any individual at the price of one penny per pound of tobacco and on the condition that the usual payment would be made to the sheriff for receiving the rent.

While some improvement was made in the last half of the seventeenth century in the collection of quitrents, the sum was never very great; and according to one report in 1696 no land had been taken over by the colony because of failure to pay the rent. As to the amount being collected near the end of the century, the figure was not impressive. For the period of six years between 1684 and 1690, the estimate has been made that receipts totalled £4,375 13s. 9d. or a little over £700 as an average for each year during this period. The figure was little changed near the end of the century, for it was reported in 1697 that the amount collected from quitrents did not total more than £800.

These weaknesses and abuses of the Virginia land system underwent a detailed analysis near the end of the seventeenth century by the newly created agency—the Lords Commissioners of Trade and Plantations which was commonly known as the Board of Trade. During the first year of its organization in 1696 the Board received a report from Edward Randolph, sent from England to be surveyor-general of customs in America. Randolph pondered the question as to why the colony of Virginia was not more densely populated with all of the migration that had occurred. He attributed little importance to the imputation of "the unhealthiness of the place" and to the assertion that tobacco sales yielded little return in England after all fees were paid. In an incisive statement he concluded that

... the chief and only reason is that the inhabitants have been and still are discouraged and hindered from planting tobacco in that colony; and servants are not so willing to go there as formerly because the members of Council and others who make an interest in the government have from time to time procured grants of very large tracts of land, so that for many years there has been no waste land to be taken up by those who bring with them servants, or by servants who have served their time. But the land has been taken up and engrossed beforehand, whereby such people are forced to hire and pay rent for lands or to go to the utmost bounds of the colony for land exposed to danger....

Randolph then reviewed the steps by which a land patent was obtained and analyzed the conditions which a person was supposed to fulfill in order to obtain the land title in fee simple. The first of these was the requirement for the annual quitrent of one shilling for fifty acres; but according to Randolph, the colonists "never pay a penny of quit-rent to the King for it, by which in strictness of law their land is forfeited." The second requirement was for seating the land within three years to prevent it from being relinquished as deserted land. The following description was given of this condition:

By seating land is meant that they build a house upon and keep a good stock of hogs and cattle, and servants to take care of them and to improve and plant the land. But instead thereof, they cut down a few trees and make thereof a hut, covering it with the bark, and turn two or three hogs into the woods by it. Or else they are to clear one acre of that land and plant and tend it for one year. But they fell twenty or thirty trees and put a little Indian corn into the ground among them as they lie and sometimes make a beginning to serve it, but take no care of their crop, nor make any further use of the land.

The third condition pertained to the keeping of "four able men well armed" on land that was situated on the frontier of the colony. Again Randolph reported that

... this law is never observed. These grants are procured upon such easy terms and very often upon false certificates of rights. Many hold twenty or thirty thousand acres of land apiece, very largely surveyed, without paying one penny of quit-rent for it. In many patents there is double the quantity of land expressed in the patent, whereby some hundred thousand acres of land are taken up but not planted, which drives away the inhabitants and servants brought up only to planting to seek their fortunes in Carolina and other places, which depopulates the country and prevents the making of many thousand hogsheads of tobacco, to the great diminution of the revenue.

Three proposals were submitted to the Board of Trade by Randolph to correct the evils of the land system: first, order a survey in every Virginia county of the lands in question; second, demand full payment of all quitrents in arrears and use legal compulsion to collect them; and third, limit grants to 500 acres for one man and have them issued on "more certain terms." Such requirements would produce threefold advantages to the crown and the colony. They would either bring in additional revenue by collection of the quitrent; or if payment were not made, approximately 100,000 acres of land would revert to the King and could be granted to new settlers. Limitation of grants to 500 acres would increase the number of planters, make settlements more compact, and produce more tobacco. And finally, both trade and the customs collection on tobacco would be enhanced.

Before concluding his report, Randolph acknowledged both the awareness of the problem and the efforts of correction initiated by Francis Nicholson while Lieutenant-Governor of Virginia from 1690 to 1692. Nicholson was

... very sensible of the damage and injustice done to the crown by their using and conniving at such unwarrantable practices in granting away the King's lands, and was resolved to reform them by suing some of the claimers for arrears of quit-rents; but finding that the Council and many of the Burgesses, among others, were concerned, and being uncertain of his continuing in the government, he ordered to begin with Laurence Smyth, who was seised of many thousand acres of land in different counties, and for one particular tract of land was indebted £80 for arrears of quit-rents, which sum after the cause was ripe for judgment, was compounded for less than one half.

Before the year was out, the Board of Trade sought more information on this problem and directed a series of searching questions in October, 1696, to Randolph who had then returned to England. Both the questions and the answers are recorded in the *Calendar of State Papers, Colonial Series, America and West Indies*, 1696-1697 (pages 172, 188-89). Out of the ten questions asked, the following seem most significant in revealing Randolph's evaluation of the Virginia land system.

What proportion of land in Virginia already taken up is now cultivated as near as you can judge?

There is in Virginia, at a moderate computation, about 500,000 acres granted by patents, of which not above 40,000 acres are cultivated and improved; besides many thousand acres of waste land high up in the country.

Why have not the prosecutions, neglected in Colonel Nicholson's time, been continued since?

Colonel Nicholson was the first Governor of Virginia who directed prosecutions for arrears of quit-rents, beginning with Colonel Laurence Smith. The case was ready for trial but the Governor came to England, and the case was afterwards compounded for a small matter.

Have any parcels of land been seized for the King's use, for want of planting or failure to pay quit-rents?

Small parcels of land are granted away every court for not being planted or seated according to law, but no land has at any time been seized to the King's use for not paying of quit-rents.

Are negro servants included in the persons who, if imported, make "rights" to grant of land. [?]

Negro servants give a right to land to those who import them, who thereupon take up land, contrary to the true intention of seating the country; but the practice being general, to the advantage of certain persons, no notice is taken of it.

Have you ever known of false certificates of rights, and how have the parties guilty thereof been punished?

I have heard of many false certificates of rights; the practice is common but little regarded, being of no prejudice to any private person.

If your methods be followed, in what county should a beginning be made?

... if my proposals were adopted, I answer that the members of Council have large tracts of land in most of the counties, for which they are in great arrears of quit-rent. It is advisable to make a beginning with some of them and to empower a person uninterested in the county to demand the arrears due to the King. These will amount to a considerable sum and will increase the King's revenue in Virginia yearly. If the patentees refuse to pay the arrears, some hundred thousand acres of land will revert to the crown, to be more carefully disposed of in future.

The Board of Trade continued the search for additional opinions about the land system in Virginia. Questions were asked individually of Henry Hartwell, a Councilor of Virginia, and Edward Chilton, Attorney-General in Virginia from 1691 to 1694. Then Hartwell and Chilton collaborated with James Blair, Councilor and Commissary of the Anglican Church in Virginia, in preparing a report that was received by the Board in October, 1697, under the title *An Account of the Present State & Government of Virginia.* The three authors of the report were English or Scottish born and represented essentially the same point of view of royal appointees who became residents of the colony and who favored an extensive use of royal authority. All three had married into Virginia families and had had numerous occasions for observation. The report reflected a greater concern for royal revenue than for the internal development of the colony, and it definitely displayed the bias of the three men, particularly Blair, against Governor Andros.

Their comments on the land system confirmed some of the conditions as set forth by Randolph's report. Stating that the country was "ill peopled" despite the headright system, they explained that "The first great abuse of this design arose from the ignorance and knavery of surveyors, who often gave out drafts of surveys without even coming on the land. They gave their descripton [sic] by some natural bounds and were sure to allow large measure, that so the persons for whom they surveyed should enjoy much larger tracts than they paid quit-rents for." The issuing of certificates for rights by the courts and secretary's office had been abused, especially the latter "which was and still is a constant mint of those rights, where they may be purchased at from one shilling to five shillings *per* right." And in another criticism of the land system, the authors concluded that the "Fundamental error of letting the King's land run away to lie waste, together with another of not seating in townships, is the cause that Virginia to-day is so ill peopled."

The Board of Trade considered reforms to correct the existing evils of the land system. Questions about these evils were posed to

Sir Edmund Andros, Governor of Virginia from 1692 to 1698; but his answers were either evasive or otherwise unsatisfactory. Francis Nicholson was then returned to the colony as Governor in 1698 with instructions for a "new method of granting land in Virginia." To prevent land from being patented without being cultivated, to encourage trade, and to increase royal revenue, land title was not to be obtained "by merely importing or buying of servants"; rather anyone who would seat and plant vacant lands was to receive 100 acres for himself and the same amount for each laborer that was brought in or for whom arrangements were made for importation within three years. The annual quitrent was to be two shillings for 100 acres provided the full number of laborers were brought in within the three-year period; if, however, full compliance had not been made, ten shillings was to be paid annually for each 100 acres for which there was no worker or the size of the grant was to be reduced proportionally. On the other hand, if the number of laborers, including members of the family, was increased beyond the original number proposed, the owner was entitled to an additional 100 acres for each extra worker.

Governor Nicholson was instructed to "consider and advise with the Council and Assembly" about putting these proposals into effect and about overcoming any difficulties that might exist because of the current laws of the colony. But instructions to the royal Governor was one thing; putting these instructions into effect was quite another. Neither the Council nor the Burgesses were willing to grapple directly with land reform and no action was taken by the two bodies to implement the recommendations of the Board of Trade. Governor Nicholson on his own ordered that no more headrights be issued for the importation of Negroes. As to the sale of headrights by the secretary's office which Nicholson found to be still prevalent, the practice was not eliminated completely. As a substitute measure which arose over the problem of land taken up in Pamunkey Neck and on the south side of Blackwater Swamp, the Governor and Council in 1699 authorized the acquisition of land by "treasury right," stating that title to fifty acres of land would be granted for the payment of five shillings sterling to the auditor. Thus during the terminal year of this study, we find the significant reappearance of sale of land by "treasury right" which increased in importance as the eighteenth century progressed. Grant by head-right continued immediately to account for the great majority of land patents issued, but after the first quarter of the eighteenth century it gradually fell into disuse.

Being unable to inaugurate the proposed plan for land reform of the Board of Trade, Nicholson turned to the improvement of collection of quitrents as the most feasible means of achieving the approximate goal. Payment of rent was an acknowledged requirement, even though frequently evaded in the seventeenth century; and Nicholson proposed a stringent collection of quitrents in arrears in order to force the return of unused land to be patented by others who would actually occupy and cultivate the vacant areas. Improvements were made in the sale of tobacco received as quitrents, and the rent roll of 1704/05 was an improvement over previous ones. Yet many loopholes still existed in the system, and Nicholson's attempts to make further reforms were hindered by the arguments that ensued with leading Councilors. His second term as executive for Virginia came to an end in 1705.

CHAPTER FIVE

The Northern Neck

Before completing this study of seventeenth-century land grants, a brief analysis will be made of the nature of the land system in the Northern Neck with some attention given to the major ways in which it differed from the remainder of Virginia. The included area reached from the Potomac River south to the Rappahannock River and from the headwaters of these two streams in the western part of the colony to Chesapeake Bay.

The separate provision for the area went back to the days of exile in France of Charles II following the execution of Charles I in 1649. As a reward to those cavaliers who had been faithful to the Stuart regime, Charles II exercised his royal prerogative by making a grant of the portions of tidewater Virginia that were not seated. In the year of the execution the Northern Neck was granted to the following seven supporters of the King: Lord John Culpeper, Lord Ralph Horton, Lord Henry Jermyn, Sir John Berkeley, Sir William Morton, Sir Dudley Wyatt, and Thomas Culpeper. Efforts of the representatives of this group were frustrated in Virginia by the suspension of royal government, and therefore the proprietary charter was ineffective for a time. It had, however, been recorded in chancery in 1649 and was revived after the restoration of Charles II to the throne. In 1662 and again in 1663 Charles II ordered the Governor and Council of Virginia to assist the proprietors in "settling the plantations and receiving the rents and profits thereof." But portions of the area had been seated since 1645, and legal obstructions were brought forth by Virginia planters and the Council to defeat the efforts of the proprietors.

A second appeal to the King led to a solution maneuvered in part by the Virginia resident agent in London, Francis Moryson. The original patent of 1649 was surrendered and a new charter was issued on May 8, 1669, to the Earl of St. Albans, Lord John Berkeley, Sir William Morton, and John Trethewy. The new document required the recognition of grants in the Northern Neck made by the Governor and Council prior to September 29, 1661, and it limited the title of the proprietors to that land which would be planted and inhabited within twenty-one years. The political jurisdiction of the area was still under the Virginia government. The laws of the colony were to remain operative, and in effect the grant was "to create a subordinate fief or proprietorship within Virginia." But considerable confusion prevailed over the retroactive recognition of grants, and many landholders sought confirmation of their ownership. "Besides there are many other grants," stated Governor William Berkeley, "in that patent inconsistent with the settlednesse of this government which hath no barr to its prosperitie but proprieties on both hands, and therefore is it mightily wounded in this last, nor have I ever observed anything so much move the peoples' griefe or passion, or which doth more put a stop to theire industry than their uncertainty whether they should make a country for the King or other proprietors."

The confusion that existed was further confounded by the grant of Charles II on February 25, 1672/73, of all of Virginia for thirty-one years to Lord Arlington and to Lord Thomas Culpeper, son of one of the original patentees of the Northern Neck by the same name. These two proprietors of the whole colony were to control all lands, collect rents, including all rents and profits in arrears since 1669, and exercise authority that sprang from grants previously made. Up until 1669 amid all the controversy over control of the Northern Neck, grants were regularly made by the local government on the basis of headrights as revealed in the land patent books. After that date the number decreased; and in March, 1674/75, the first land grant of 5,000 acres, later George Washington's Mount Vernon, was issued to Nicholas Spencer and John Washington of Westmoreland in the name of the proprietors with the common seal being affixed to the grant by Thomas Culpeper and Anthony Trethewy. By this date Thomas Culpeper had obtained from the proprietors of 1669 recognition of one-sixth interest in the Northern Neck for him and his cousin on the basis of their fathers having been original patentees.

Opposition to the proprietary grant of the Northern Neck in Virginia led to efforts of the Assembly, encouraged by Governor William Berkeley, to buy out the rights of the proprietors. Apparently the proprietors were willing to sell and set the price of £400 each for the six shares then held in the charter. Negotiations to complete the transaction were interrupted by the outbreak of Bacon's Rebellion, and the status of the proprietary grant hung in suspension. Meanwhile, Thomas, Lord Culpeper was appointed Governor of Virginia but did not arrive in the colony until 1680. The next year Culpeper bought up the proprietary rights in Virginia, both the rights of the other proprietors in the Northern Neck and the rights of Lord Arlington for all of Virginia. In 1684, however, he gave up the Arlington charter of 1673 to the crown in return for an annual pension of £600 for twenty-one years.

Lord Culpeper retained the Northern Neck charter and made efforts to encourage settlement of the area. But the terminal date of the twenty-one year period stipulated in the charter of 1669 was approaching, and he appealed for a renewal of the grant on the basis that the amount of land intended by Charles II had not been taken up. Considering the restriction an impracticable one, King James II issued a new charter in 1688 with Lord Culpeper as the sole proprietor and with no time limit specified. Through changes and additions prompted by Culpeper's knowledge of Virginia's geography, the area of the grant included in the Northern Neck was substantially enlarged over the boundaries stated in the previous charters of 1649 and 1669, the additions later being interpreted as extending Culpeper's claim beyond the Blue Ridge Mountains to the foot of the Alleghenies. The area as outlined in 1688 was as follows with the additions to the former descriptions shown in italics:

All that entire tract, territory or parcel of land situate, lying and being *in Virginia* in America and bounded by and within the *first* heads or *springs* of the rivers of Tappanhannocke alias Rappahanocke and Quiriough alias Patawomacke Rivers, the courses of the said rivers, *from their said first heads or springs*, as they are commonly called and known by the inhabitants and descriptions of those parts, and the Bay of Chesapoyocke, together with the said rivers themselves and all the islands within the *outermost* banks thereof, *and the soil of all and singular the premisses.*

Soon after receiving this third charter, Lord Culpeper died on January 27, 1688/89. Despite efforts that were again made by the colony to eliminate the proprietary grant, it was confirmed to Culpeper's survivors and passed by marriage to the Fairfax family.

After the 1669 charter, the proprietors opened an office in the colony and an agent was designated to handle land grants and collect fees. The scant records that survive indicate that from 1670 to 1673, Thomas Kirton was agent in the land office in Northumberland; from 1673 to 1677, William Aretkin was appointed the proprietor's "agent in Virginia"; and from 1677 to 1689, Daniel Parke and Nicholas Spencer were agents in the land office in Westmoreland.

Beginning in 1690 land patents in the Northern Neck were entered separately and the grant books that have survived give a good account of the land policy under the proprietors. Philip Ludwell served as agent from 1690 to 1693 and began an orderly handling of the proprietor's interest at the land office in Westmoreland. Throughout his term as agent he used a form for land grants in establishing his authority which reviewed a part of the checkered history of the Northern Neck. The introductory portion of this form was as follows:

Whereas King Charles the Seacond of ever blessed memory by his letters pattents under the broad seale of England beareing date at Westminister the eighth day of May in the one and twentyeth yeare of his reigne Annoqe Dom. 1669, His Matie was gratiously pleased to give graunt and confirme unto Henry then Earle of St. Albons, John Lord Berkley, Sir William Morton, Knt., & John Trethewy, Esqr., there heires & assignes all that intire tract territory or parcell of land lyinge & being betweene the two rivers of Rapah. and Patomack and the courses of the said rivers and the Bay of Chesapeake, as by the said graunts, recourse beinge had there unto, will more at large appeare, and

Whereas all the rite and title of in and to the said lands & premisses is by deed enrold and other suffentient conveyance in law conveyed and made over to Thomas Lord Culpeper, eldest sonn & heire of John late Lord Culpeper, his heires & assignes for ever, who is thereby become sole owner and propriator of the said land in fee symple, and

Whereas Kinge James the Seacond hath beene gratiously pleased by his letters pattents bearinge date at Westminister the 27th day of September 1688, and in the fourth yeare of his Maties. reigne, to confirme the said graunt for the said tract or parcell of land to the said Thomas Lord Culpeper his heires & assignes for ever, as by the said graunt, relation beinge there unto had, will more at large appeare

And the said Thomas Lord Culpeper he beinge since deceased all the rite title and interest of in and to the said tract of land lawfully desendinge on the Honorble. Mrs. Katherine Culpeper sole daughter and heire of the said Thomas late Lord Culpeper, and Allexander Culpeper Esqr. who cometh in part propriator by lawfull conveyance from Thomas late Lord Culpeper, and confirmed by the said Mrs. Katherine Culpeper, who are thereby now become the true and lawfull propriators of the said tract or territory, and

Whereas the said propriators have thought fitt under there hands & seales to depute me Phillip Ludwell Esqr. with full power and authority to act in the prmisses. persuant to the powers granted by there said Maties. as fully & amply to all intents & purposes as they the said propriators them selves might or could doe if they were personally present,

NOW KNOW YEE therefore....

The provisions in the fourth paragraph above designating Mrs. Katherine Culpeper and Alexander Culpeper as "the true and lawfull propriators" were obsolete after the former married Lord Fairfax while Ludwell was still agent. By law the husband also became a proprietor and should have been added to the list. This omission was corrected by George Brent and William Fitzhugh, the two agents who succeeded Ludwell in 1693 and continued to serve during the 1690's in the land office at Woodstock in Stafford County. In a much simplified form, Brent and Fitzhugh merely listed the proprietors including the husband as follows:

Margarett Lady Culpeper, Thomas Lord Fairfax, Katherine his wife and Alexander Culpeper Esquire, proprietors of the Northern Neck of Virginia....

The grants made by the various agents of the proprietors in the Northern Neck were not substantially different in nature from those held under a Virginia land patent. Both tenures reflected the feudal law of the manor. The proprietors held their land in free and common socage, and the planters in the Northern Neck paid quitrents and fees to the proprietors rather than to the crown.

While the nature of the tenure was similar, there was a marked difference in the methods of obtaining a grant. Instead of the headright which we have seen was the basis for Virginia land grants during most of the seventeenth century, the proprietors turned to what they considered the more practical procedure—acquisition of title by purchase, or the "treasury right." To obtain title to land the individual paid a "composition" which was established at a uniform rate. For each 100 acres in grants less than 600, the price was five shillings; for 100 acres in grants more than 600, the price was increased to ten shillings. Payment was permitted in tobacco which was valued at the rate of six shillings for every 100 pounds in 1690. Such a provision could permit the acquisition of large holdings without the manipulations that were practiced under the headright system.

In the provision for quitrents, the two areas were similar. The amount of the quitrent in the Northern Neck was the same as elsewhere in Virginia—two shillings annually for 100 acres. Under agents Brent and Fitzhugh one exception occurred with the attempt in 1694 to double the quitrent and thereby maintain the same scale as was customary in Maryland at the time. But few grants have been found to indicate the agents succeeded to any extent in establishing the higher rate.

Relative to requirements for seating to validate the claim, the two areas followed a different course as the seventeenth century progressed. We have previously noted the three-year "seating and planting" requirement for other Virginia patents. Similar provisions were included in the first proprietary grants as revealed in the earliest patent in 1675. But beginning with the grant for Brent Town in 1687, the seating requirement was omitted and this precedent was followed for all subsequent proprietary grants in the Northern Neck in the seventeenth and eighteenth centuries.

For the seventeenth century under consideration in this study, there was considerable private and public animosity displayed toward the principles of the proprietary system. There was a distrust of the grants that were issued, and there was criticism of the proprietary system as it differed from the remainder of Virginia. Demand for land in the area was not as great; and with the exception of large holdings such as that of William Fitzhugh, most of the patents were small. It was not until the eighteenth century that public antipathy toward the proprietors was for the most part dispelled and that demands on the Northern Neck land offices increased to equal other areas in Virginia.

RETROSPECT

The availability of land was a leading motive in the European colonization of America. Although much of the country was inhabited by Indians, European nations claimed sovereignty over the area and denied superior claims by the non-Christian aborigines. The London Company held essentially to this position, although gradually the colony of Virginia, like other English colonies, recognized the Indian's right of occupation and provided some compensation for relinquishment of territory. By the middle of the seventeenth century Virginia had initiated the policy of laying out Indian boundaries or creating reservations for neighboring tribes that were not open to white settlement.

Under the London Company land was held in common until the provision for distribution to individual stockholders was carried out after 1616. In addition to grants according to the number of shares of stock owned, the company rewarded individuals with land for special services rendered to the colony. And to stimulate immigration, grants were offered as dividends to voluntary associations or "societies of adventurers" for organizing and financing settlements such as the hundred or particular plantations. It was also possible to obtain patents by purchase or by "treasury right" under the company, but the most significant development was the provision for acquisition by headright as outlined in the Instructions to Governor George Yeardley in 1618.

With the dissolution of the company in 1624, the "treasury right" was discontinued in Virginia and did not reappear other than in the Northern Neck until 1699. The major method of obtaining title to land was the headright which attempted to maintain an appropriate balance between the size of the population and the area patented. However, its basic concept was distorted by irregular practices and fraudulent acts. Other conditions for obtaining patents after 1624 were as a dividend for each share of stock invested in the company, as remuneration for special services, and as a means of encouraging frontier fortification.

The size of land patents gradually increased during the seventeenth century with the peak being reached in the third quarter. During the last quarter of the period there was a definite trend toward the breakup of large estates by distribution to heirs and by sale of small segments of the larger patent. Whatever the variation in size, the small landholder constituted the major group in seventeenth-century Virginia and assumed a more important role in the socio-economic pattern of the colony than is evident from the descriptions of plantation life by romantic writers.

By the end of the seventeenth century the use of the headright as the major means of land distribution began to give way to acquisition of title by purchase in all of Virginia other than the Northern Neck. For the Northern Neck which was granted to various proprietors who were faithful to the King during the civil war, the headright never served as the basis of the land system. Rather the distribution of land by the "treasury right" was employed in the seventeenth as well as the eighteenth century.

The abuses of the land system and lax enforcement of its major principles brought forth a detailed discussion of its many facets by the Board of Trade near the end of the century. Reforms were proposed that would enhance the royal revenue by collection of the quitrent and would prevent the accumulation of large estates. But the existence of vast areas of unoccupied land on the frontier militated against the restriction, and there was considerable opposition to feudal tenures and to the payment of rents to the crown. The proposed reforms did not prevent the acquisition of large landholdings; the few large estates of the seventeenth century increased both in number and size in the eighteenth century and from them were developed the large plantations of some of the well-known Virginia leaders of the American Revolution.

BIBLIOGRAPHY

I. Manuscripts

Virginia Land Patents. Forty-two volumes. Records of the Virginia State Land Office now in the custody of the Virginia State Library, Richmond. Indispensable source for the study of land grants in Colonial Virginia. Nine volumes cover the period to 1706 with two additional volumes for the Northern Neck beginning in 1690: Northern Neck Grants No. 1, 1690-1692 and Northern Neck Grants No. 2, 1694-1700.

Thomas Jefferson Papers. Alderman Library, University of Virginia, Charlottesville.

II. Printed Primary Sources

Brown, Alexander, ed., *The Genesis of the United States*, New York: Houghton, Mifflin and Company, 1890. 2 vols.

Force, Peter, ed., *Tracts and Other Papers Relating Principally to the Origin Settlement and Progress of the Colonies in North America, from the Discovery of the Country to the Year 1776*, Washington, D.C., 1836-1846. 4 vols.

Grant, William, Munro (James) and Fitzroy (A. W.), eds., *Acts of the Privy Council of England, Colonial Series, 1613-1783*, London, 1908-1912. 6 vols.

Hartwell, Henry, Blair (James) and Chilton (Edward), *The Present State of Virginia and the College*. Edited by H. D. Farish, Williamsburg: Colonial Williamsburg, Inc., 1940.

Hening, W. W., ed., *Statutes at Large: being a Collection of All the Laws of Virginia from the First Session of the Legislature in the Year 1619 [to 1792]*. Richmond, 1809. 13 vols.

Kennedy, J. P. and McIlwaine, H. R., eds., *Journals of the House of Burgesses of Virginia, 1619-1776*, Richmond: The Colonial Press, 1905-1915. 13 vols.

Kingsbury, S. M., ed., *The Records of the Virginia Company of London*, Washington, D.C.: Government Printing Office, 1906 and 1933. 4 vols.

Labaree, L. W., ed., *Royal Instructions to British Colonial Governors, 1670-1776*, New York: D. Appleton-Century Company, 1935. 2 vols.

McIlwaine, H. R. and Hall, W. L., eds., *Executive Journals of the Council of Colonial Virginia*, Richmond: Virginia State Library, 1925.

McIlwaine, H. R., ed., *Legislative Journals of the Council of Colonial Virginia, 1680-1775*, Richmond: The Colonial Press, 1918-1919. 3 vols.

— —, *Minutes of the Council and General Court of Colonial Virginia, 1622-1632, 1670-1676*, Richmond: The Colonial Press, 1924.

Nugent, Nell M., ed., *Cavaliers and Pioneers: Abstracts of Virginia Land Patents and Grants*, Richmond: The Dietz Printing Company, 1934. Only volume I published covering the period from 1623 to 1666. Excellent source for study of seventeenth-century land grants.

Sainsbury, W. N. and others, eds., *Calendar of State Papers, Colonial Series, America and West Indies*, London, 1860-.

III. Index and Periodicals

Swem, E. G., comp., *Virginia Historical Index*, Roanoke: Stone Printing Company, 1934-1936. 2 vols.

Valuable guide to material found in Hening's *Statutes, Virginia Magazine of History and Biography, Tyler's Quarterly Historical and Genealogical Magazine, William and Mary College Quarterly Historical Magazine* — first and second series, *Calendar of Virginia State Papers ... Preserved in the Capitol at Richmond, Virginia Historical Register and Literary Adviser*, and *Lower Norfolk County Virginia Antiquary*.

IV. Secondary Sources — Books

Ames, Susie M., *Studies of the Virginia Eastern Shore in the Seventeenth Century*, Richmond: The Dietz Press, 1940.

Andrews, C, M., *The Colonial Period of American History*, New Haven: Yale University Press, 1934-1938. 4 vols.

Beverley, Robert, *The History of Virginia in Four Parts*. Reprinted from the author's second revised edition, 1722. Richmond, 1855.

Brown, Alexander, *The First Republic in America*, New York: Houghton, Mifflin and Company, 1898.

Bruce, P. A., *The Economic History of Virginia in the Seventeenth Century*, New York: Macmillan and Company, 1896. 2 vols.

— —, *Institutional History of Virginia in the Seventeenth Century*, New York: G. P. Putnam's Sons, 1910. 2 vols.

— —, *Social Life of Virginia in the Seventeenth Century: An Inquiry into the Origin of the Higher Planting Class, together with an Account of the Habits, Customs, and Diversions of the People*, Richmond: Whittet & Shepperson, 1907.

Craven, W. F., *Dissolution of the Virginia Company: The failure of a Colonial Experiment*, New York: Oxford University Press, 1932.

— —, *The Southern Colonies in the Seventeenth Century, 1607-1689*. Volume I of *A History of the South*, Baton Rouge: Louisiana State University Press, 1949.

Harrison, *Fairfax, Virginia Land Grants: A Study of Conveyancing in Relation to Colonial Politics*, Richmond: The Old Dominion Press, 1925. Valuable for its emphasis upon the Northern Neck.

Osgood, H. L., *The American Colonies in the Seventeenth Century*, New York: Macmillan Company, 1904-1907. 3 vols.

Voorhis, M. C., The Land Grant Policy of Colonial Virginia, 1607-1774, Unpublished Ph.D. dissertation, University of Virginia.

Valuable study with emphasis upon analysis of land policy. Does not include the Northern Neck.

Wertenbaker, T. J., *Patrician and Plebeian in Virginia; or, The Origin and Development of the Social Classes of the Old Dominion*, Charlottesville, 1910.

— —, *The Planters of Colonial Virginia*, Princeton: Princeton University Press, 1922.

— —, *Virginia under the Stuarts, 1607-1688*, Princeton: Princeton University Press, 1914.

Wright, L. B., *The First Gentlemen of Virginia: Intellectual Qualities of the Early Colonial Ruling Class*, San Marino: The Huntington Library, 1940.

Virginia 350th Anniversary Commission

Honorary Chairman

Thomas B. Stanley, Governor

Lewis A. Mcmurran, Jr., *Chairman of the Commission*

Members of Senate appointed by President of the Senate:

Lloyd C. Bird, Vice Chairman   Harry F. Byrd, Jr.

Edward L. Breeden, Jr.   W. Marvin Minter

Members of the House of Delegates appointed by the Speaker of the House:

Russell M. Carneal   Felix E. Edmunds

Hale Collins   Lewis A. McMurran, Jr.

John W. Cooke   W. Tayloe Murphy

Edmund T. DeJarnette   Fred G. Pollard

Members appointed by the Governor:

Miss Ellen Bagby   Carlisle H. Humelsine

Alvin D. Chandler   Verbon E. Kemp

Allen R. Matthews

Parke Rouse, Jr., *Executive Director*

The Jamestown-Williamsburg-Yorktown
Celebration Commission

Appointed by the President of the United States

Robert V. Hatcher, Chairman   Samuel M. Bemiss, Vice Chairman

Frank L. Boyden   Bentley Hite

David E. Finley   Winthrop Rockefeller

Conrad L. Wirth

Appointed by the Vice President of the United States

Harry F. Byrd   A. Willis Robertson

Appointed by the Speaker of the House of Representatives

Edward J. Robeson, Jr.   Richard H. Poff

H. K. Roberts, *Administrative Director*

FEVDIGRAPHIA.

THE SYNOPSIS

OR EPITOME OF

SVRVEYING METHODIZED.

Anatomizing the whole Corps of the Facultie; *Viz.*

The Materiall, Mathematicall, Mechanicall and
Legall Parts,
Intimating all the Incidents to Fees and Possessions, and
whatsoeuer may be comprized vnder their Matter, Forme,
Proprietie, and Valuation.
Very pertinent to be perused of all those, whom the Right, Reuenewe,
Estimation, Farming, Occupation, Manurance, Subduing,
Preparing and Imploying of Arable, Medow, Pasture, and all
other plots doe concerne.
And no lesse remarkable for all Vnder-takers in the Plantation
of Ireland or Virginia, for all Trauailers for Discoueries of
forraine Countries, and for Purchasers, Exchangers, or Sellers
of Land, and for euery other Interessee in the Profits
or Practise deriued from the compleate SVRVEY
Of Manours, Lands, Tenements, Edifices, Woods, Waters, Titles,
Tenures, Euidences, &c.
Composed in a compendious Digest by
W. Folkingham. G.

Qua prosunt singula, multaiuvant.

LONDON

Printed for *Richard Moore,* and are to be solde at his shop in Saint
Dunstanes Church-yard in Fleete-streete,
1610.

[Photograph by T. L. Williams]

THE

SVRVEIORS

DIALOGVE,

Very profitable for all men to pervse, but
especially for Gentlemen, Farmers, and Husband-
men,
that shall either haue occasion, or be willing
to buy, hire, or sell Lands: As in the ready and perfect
Surueying of them, with the manner and Method of
keeping a Court of Suruey with many necessary rules,
and familiar Tables to that purpose.
As also,
The vse of the Manuring of some Grounds, fit as well
for Lords, *as for* Tennants.

Now the third time Imprinted.

And by the same Author inlarged, and a sixt Booke newly
added, of a familiar conference, betweene a Pvrchaser,
and a Svrveyor of Lands; of the true vse of both being
very needfull for all such as are to purchase Land,
whether it be in Fee simple, or by Lease.

Diuided into sixe Bookes by I. N.

Prov. 17.2.

*A discreate Seruant shall haue rule ouer an vnthriftie Sonne, and he shall
deuide the heritage among the brethren.*

Voluntas pro facultate.

LONDON:

Printed by Thomas Snodham. 1618.

[Photograph by T. L. Williams]